LINCOLN CHRISTIAN COLLEGE AND S

*In his book **Weathering the Midlife Storm**, Bobb Biehl demonstrates again that God has gifted him with an awareness, a perspective, and a vantage point to pinpoint the subtle; to snapshoot the hidden; to expose the secluded truths that serve to set us free. Read and be released to be all you were created to be.*

BILL MCCARTNEY
*Founder*
*Promise Keepers*

# WEATHERING THE MIDLIFE STORM

## BOBB BIEHL

COMPLETE AND UNABRIDGED

Since 1948, The Book Club You Can Trust

Unless otherwise indicated, all Scripture references are from the *Holy Bible, New International Version®*. Copyright © 1973, 1978, 1984 by International Bible Society. Used by permission of Zondervan Publishing House. All rights reserved.

Editor: Barbara Williams
Design: Scott Rattray
Cover Illustration: Barton Stabler
Interior Maps: Andrea Boven

ISBN: 1-56476-583-0
Suggested Subject Heading: PERSONAL GROWTH

© 1996 by Bobb Biehl. All rights reserved.
Printed in the United States of America.

1  2  3  4  5  6  7  8  9  10  Printing/Year  00  99  98  97  96

No part of this book may be reproduced in any form without written permission, except for brief quotations in books and critical reviews. For information write Victor Books, 1825 College Avenue,

First hardcover edition for Christian Family Book Club: 1997

# CONTENTS

99308

# *Dedication*

I would like to dedicate this book
to all of the family members,
friends and
advisers
whose understanding, prayers, and wise council
helped me
Weather my MIDLIFE STORM!

Thank you each and every one.

Bobb

# Introduction

## THE MIDLIFE HOPE

Imagine with me that you are on a small northern Michigan farm. There's a little farmhouse and a barn a short distance away with some livestock inside. It's winter and snow has been falling in large flakes for hours.

A gentle breeze begins to blow,
   the snow swirls gently around the end of the house . . . quietly. . . .
The wind increases, whistling its way into your home,
   whistling through the smallest cracks,
     becoming a blizzard of tiny pieces of snow
      and wind . . .
        blinding whiteness . . .
          seeing nothing out the window . . .
           feeling trapped . . .
             not knowing when the
              blizzard will end.

You think, plenty of food . . .
   plenty of fuel . . .
     set for at least ten days . . .
      relax in the warm comfort of home.

But, what if it lasts longer?
  What if you run out of food, or fuel . . .
    or possibly freeze to death . . .
      It'll be OK . . . won't it?

The animals!
  You have to feed the animals in the barn . . .
    bundle up as best you can,
      open the door . . . can't even see the barn!

Stepping outside into a blinding blizzard . . .
  an immediate sense of disorientation
    as intense cold slaps you in the face . . .
      deafening, howling wind . . .
      trapped in the violent forces of nature.

Can't think . . .
  What do you do?
    Which way do you go?
      You could literally freeze to death in your own yard!
        Help! You must get some help!

You turn to look at the house a few feet behind you,
  and you lose a sense of north
    and south . . .you are lost . . .
      far from the barn . . . need a rope . . .
        you are totally disoriented, lost, fearful for your life,
          hesitant to go one step more in any direction
            because it may be away from the home
              and not toward it.

Everything is equally white . . .
  a few degrees off and you could miss the house
    by two or three feet and never realize it . . .
      and then wander as many have . . .
        for the rest of life, lost in a blizzard.

You yell, but it seems that no one hears over the wind.
  Then you remember that what you really need is a rope

tied to both the house and the barn.
    Something to give you an objective sense
      of where you have been,
        where you are,
          and where you are going.

Do the feelings of being lost—even trapped—seem familiar to you? Does your life feel a lot like a blizzard? Do you sometimes sense a lack of direction, disorientation, confusion, indecision, fear, or hopelessness? This book can be the objective rope in your midlife struggle, giving you a guide to get safely out of the blizzard. It will help you discover a crystal-clear context for your life, understand what you are experiencing, and provide you with a step-by-step process to decide your next steps. It can help you find hope.

# A BLIZZARD AND MIDLIFE COMPARISON

*A blinding snow blizzard*
Snow: tiny flakes, any one
of which is very manageable,
but the accumulation becomes
very dangerous.

*A midlife emotional blizzard*
Small questions, ideas,
fears, dreams, concerns, any
one of which is very manageable,
but the accumulation becomes
very dangerous.

Wind: what drives the little
flakes.

Pace: what drives the multitude
of ideas, fears, etc.

Blurred vision: when the wind
drives the pieces of snow to the
point where you no longer see the
landscape clearly.

Blurred vision: when your
schedule drives the pieces of your
life to the point where you no
longer see the future clearly.

You begin to feel trapped, lost,
disoriented. You can't tell north
from south.

You begin to feel trapped, lost,
disoriented. You can't tell which
way leads you out of the
emotional blizzard and which
way leads you into deeper
disorientation.

A blizzard is seasonal—it only
comes in winter. But, when it
hits, it is hard to imagine it won't
last forever.

Midlife is a season—it comes in
the thirties, forties, fifties. But
when it hits, it is hard to imagine
that it won't last forever.

It occurs to you that you could
actually die in this blizzard!

It occurs to you that you could
actually die in this emotional
blizzard, or be trapped in it for
the rest of your life.

You yell, but no one hears.

You try to explain what it feels
like, but no one understands.

You need a rope to guide you.

You need an objective process to
guide you to clear thinking and
emotional safety.

A rope.

This book.

Midlife feels like an emotional blizzard. Some of the swirling, disorienting confusion in your mind may be created by questions like:

Am I stuck here for the "rest of my life"?

Is this how it feels to get "old"?

Is anything worth it?

Will I ever drive a race car, like I've always wanted?

Why can't you understand me? Why can't I understand myself?

Will I ever get the promotion? Do I even really want it?

Where has all of my former confidence gone?

When I'm old, will I become just like my mother/father?

Why do I feel so very, very lonely—even when I have lots of friends?

Why does God feel so distant, so uncaring, so silent?

Are my kids ever going to get out of their troubles?

Did I really marry the right person in the first place?

Is this lump on my body cancer? Should I have it checked? Or am I just being paranoid?

These questions, and thousands like them, may begin to form small, disjointed fragments which drift in your mind unanswered or even unaddressed because of the frantic pace we all keep in the busy midlife years. And little by little, these unanswered questions can create a blur in your thinking.

If this is true for you, STOP RIGHT NOW, get to your favorite writing instrument (pen, pencil, computer, Dictaphone, etc.), and begin to make as exhaustive a list as you are able of the unanswered questions swirling about in your mind today.

THIS BOOK WAS WRITTEN TO HELP YOU MAKE SENSE OF THESE QUESTIONS!

Since 1976 I have invested more than 20,000 hours behind the defenses of healthy executives. Almost nothing shocks me anymore. I have counseled individuals, their mates and families, and even their friends in the throes of midlife confusion. I have listened for hundreds and thousands of hours while people lost in their own emotional blizzards have opened up their hearts and poured out the questions and concerns hidden deep inside. I have heard the pain. I have seen the tragedy.

But after years of dealing with the midlife issues of healthy, normal, adult leaders, I have reached a conclusion. The midlife years are not as unique as they feel. Others have been where you now are! There is a very specific pattern, or progression, in the midlife process. Once you really understand the process, you'll also understand that you and those you love are not condemned to wander in emotional circles for the rest of your life.

There is a framework, a process, a pathway, a map out of the midlife confusion. I call it THE MIDLIFE MAP, and it will enable you to successfully weather your own midlife storm. There is hope!

This book has been written assuming that you are somewhere in the midlife blizzard. It provides an objective framework—a map—for you or for anyone who is trying to relate to you. It will help you:

- Navigate around the midlife rocks on which so many great leaders have met their destruction;
- Work through the Midlife Reevaluation phase;
- Consider alternatives to the Midlife Crisis and Dropout phases.

It will also help:

- Your mate as he/she relates to your struggles;
- Your counselors/advisers as they try to create next steps for your journey;
- Your parents as they try to understand where you are right now.

To your mate, your counselors, your parents, and anyone else trying to understand where you are, I offer this simple proverb:

Be slow
to judge the person in a midlife blizzard,
before you yourself
have been trapped
in a place where you feel totally disoriented
by hundreds of unanswered questions
floating in your head and your heart.
Bobb Biehl

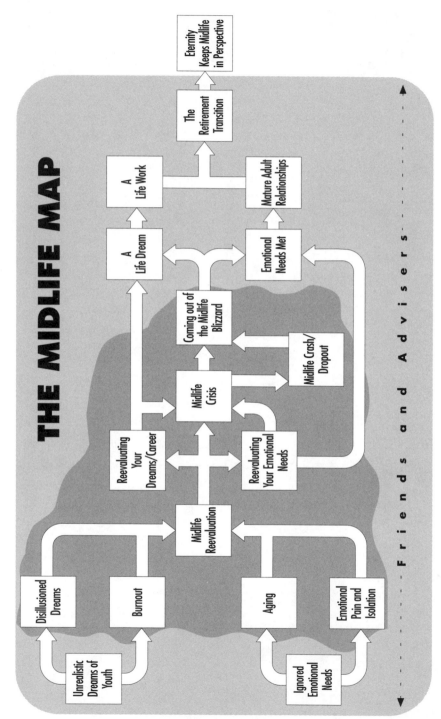

THE MIDLIFE MAP

Unrealistic Dreams of Youth

Disillusioned Dreams

Burnout

Midlife Reevaluation

Reevaluating Your Dreams/Career

Midlife Crisis

Coming out of the Midlife Blizzard

A Life Dream

A Life Work

The Retirement Transition

Eternity Keeps Midlife in Perspective

Reevaluating Your Emotional Needs

Midlife Crash/ Dropout

Emotional Needs Met

Mature Adult Relationships

Aging

Emotional Pain and Isolation

Ignored Emotional Needs

Friends and Advisers

© Bobb Biehl 1993

# The Midlife Map

*The Midlife Map provides a context to help you identify exactly where you are in the midlife process.*

You are lost unless you know where you are. But how do you know where you are? You only know where you are because of a context. Context can be a simple road map, a wiring diagram, a grid, a line on a chart, a model, a time line, a budget. Context is a "big picture" look at the whole that helps each piece of the whole make sense.

Let's say while driving at night, you take a few wrong turns, and conclude that you are completely lost. You have never been in this area before. You dig around in the rental car glove compartment and find an area map. You come to a crossroad and see signs reading State Road 88 and U.S. 131. You look on the map. Bingo! You are no longer lost. You experience great emotional relief! You knew without a map that you were in the United States of America. You knew you were in the state of Michigan. But with the help of the map you soon found that you were in Antrim county, in the village of Mancelona.

Now, with this information you can retrace your route a few miles and get back on track. Everything seemed confusing, even disorienting, without a context. But now that your context is clear, you are no longer lost. Does that make sense?

So, what is the context for midlife? What does the big picture look like? And where can you find a map to show you precisely where you have been, where you are today, and where you are likely headed tomorrow? In the pages that follow, you will walk through the Map

Points of the Midlife Map to personal, mental, and emotional clarity and freedom.

In this chapter I introduce you to the Midlife Map, the context for addressing the confusion of the midlife years. This map describes each Map Point in the midlife process, and becomes the framework for each of the succeeding chapters.

Study the diagram on page 16 carefully, to get a feel for how the pieces fit together in this Midlife Map. Then follow along as we take a brief Map Point-by-Map Point overview.

## Map Point 1: Friends and Advisers

It helps to remember that you have friends and advisers who are outside your blizzard. Some may not understand what you're experiencing, but they can provide objective perspective on your life today and affirm your worth. These are people—spouse, friends, parents, therapists, mentors—who love you, who care about you, who want to help.

(Map Point 1 is your primary source of objective help in working your way through the midlife storm. The Midlife Map gives you a path to follow. Your "significant others" are your support system.)

## Map Point 2: Unrealistic Dreams of Youth

Prior to midlife you may have had inspirational dreams for your future. Many of these dreams were unrealistic, but they were (and perhaps still are) very energizing.

## Map Point 3: Ignored Emotional Needs

Prior to midlife you also probably had unmet emotional needs. In the process of surviving and succeeding in your career you may have tended to ignore these needs. For example, you may have assumed that your need to be loved, respected, appreciated, or secure would be met if only you could reach your goals.

(Map Points 2 and 3 represent the two fundamental issues we struggle with in midlife—our life dreams and emotional needs.)

## Map Point 4: Disillusioned Dreams: The First Midlife Reevaluation "Trigger"

In your late thirties or early forties—depending on who you are and your circumstances—the dream disillusionment process begins. You realize that your dreams may have been illusions and that perhaps you

will never achieve what you originally thought you would. You begin questioning who you are, where you're going, what you're worth.

## Map Point 5: Burnout: The Second Midlife Reevaluation "Trigger"

When you try so hard, for so long, to reach certain dreams that you can't seem to achieve, your natural energy gets exhausted and you find you're working on forced energy alone. You may begin to wonder if it's worth the effort.

## Map Point 6: Aging: The Third Midlife Reevaluation "Trigger"

The aging process affects everyone, and when you begin to notice it gaining on you, thousands of questions begin to surface: "Am I slowing down, already? Am I still attractive? Am I finished? Can I face growing old without realizing my dreams? Am I going to end up like my parents?"

## Map Point 7: Emotional Pain and Isolation: The Fourth Midlife Reevaluation "Trigger"

The combination of having ignored your emotional needs and the aging process may stimulate many new questions: "Will my needs ever be met? I've been giving to other people all my life, when is someone going to love me? Will I ever truly be respected? When will I finally feel secure?"

Map Points 4, 5, 6, and 7 are the four primary "triggers" setting in motion your personal midlife reevaluation. This "Midlife Blizzard" into which you may be entering encompasses a unique time of your life. It is a time when you have all of these unanswered (and seemingly unanswerable!) questions floating around in your head and your heart. And, your personal schedule is so demanding that you can't really stop and solve or answer them.

## Map Point 8: Midlife Reevaluation

Reevaluation is a very healthy, helpful process in which you identify the changes necessary in your life to address the two fundamental issues of midlife: your unrealized dreams and your unmet emotional needs. Some people are able to enter this process one question at a time. But for others it can lead to emotional collapse, physical illness, or unpredictable behavior.

Map Point 8 is the first of three stages of the Midlife Process: (1) Midlife Reevaluation, (2) Midlife Crisis, and (3) Midlife Crash/Dropout. There is hope (even a high likelihood) that Midlife Crisis, and Midlife

Crash/Dropout can be successfully avoided if the reevaluation questions are answered properly.

## Map Point 9: Reevaluating Your Dreams/Career

Here is where we begin to reassess the possibility of dreaming a new dream, starting a new position, or even starting an entirely new career. You have two fundamental choices at this point: You can recognize your need for a dream and a career that fits you and bypass all the other midlife issues (and go to Map Point 14), or you can drift toward Midlife Crisis (Map Point 11).

## Map Point 10: Reevaluating Your Emotional Needs

Identify your unmet emotional needs and develop new ways of meeting your emotional needs. Begin by asking: "What do I really need from people?" As with #9, you have two choices: Either identify your unmet emotional needs and get them met (and proceed to Map Point 16), or you can go into Midlife Crisis (Map Point 11).

(The questions asked in *both* Map Points 9 and 10 must be answered to your personal satisfaction to avoid a midlife crisis.)

## Map Point 11: Midlife Crisis

Midlife crisis happens when you pass the threshold of core values, and say, "Regardless of the consequences, I will have what or whom I need." The consequences of unresolved career questions and unmet emotional needs are often chaos, futility, broken promises, broken relationships, greater self-doubt, compounded unmet needs. But the pain of unmet emotional needs and not having a dream you can believe in is so powerful that it seems worth the risk.

## Map Point 12: Midlife Crash/Dropout

In midlife crisis you think something new is going to help, but it doesn't. You try regardless of the consequences, and still nothing helps. Pretty soon you simply get tired of trying and say, "I quit; I've had enough; I can't do this anymore; I'm out of here." This is where some people put out their thumb and hitchhike their way into oblivion, becoming street people and joining the ranks of the homeless. Some people drop out emotionally and never compete at work again. Others drop out relationally, and stop talking to their former friends, for years—or for life. Dropping out is often characterized by isolation, loneliness, emptiness, hopelessness, emotional numbness, or sometimes anger and vengeance.

## Map Point 13: Coming Out of the Midlife Blizzard

Often it takes three to five, or even as much as ten years, to regain a sense of life balance after a midlife crisis or crash. New careers or new relationships may have been initiated during the midlife blizzard that over the course of time help restore a sense of life balance. However, this is not automatic. Many people are still stuck in midlife issues into their sixties and seventies. Giving up on their dreams and denying their legitimate needs results in their ending life with a whimper rather than a bang.

## Map Point 14: A Life Dream

This is where you define your new motivating dreams or simply revise existing ones to fit reality.

## Map Point 15: A Life Work

Using the LifeWork Chart, you can go beyond planning your next "career move" to defining your life work in the light of your new, motivating dreams.

## Map Point 16: Emotional Needs Met

Once you have formed new relational skills, you discover healthy ways of relating to people who in turn meet your emotional needs.

## Map Point 17: Mature Adult Relationships

When you have your emotional needs met, you are able to develop and maintain healthy, balanced relationships with people over the years.

## Map Point 18: The Retirement Transition

Substituting the word "transition" for the traditional word "retirement" offers a whole new perspective on your later years. Prepare for the new life adjustments that accompany aging. Discover ways of giving to others out of your life experience.

## Map Point 19: Eternity Keeps Midlife in Perspective

Consider living your life from the perspective of eternity—a time without end. Eternity gives a unique perspective on the passing events of our lives; today is not all there is.

As you'll see, the Midlife Map can give you a basis for seeing where you are today. Are you in Midlife Reevaluation (Map Point 8)? Are you at Map Point 10, in the middle of a Midlife Crisis? Or perhaps you're at Map Point 4, just realizing that you've been disappointed in your dreams. Where are you?

The Midlife Map also gives you a basis to help friends find where they are. As you listen, ask yourself, "Where is this person?" Are they talking about their unmet emotional needs (Map Point 7)? Or are they talking about career change (Map Point 9)? The Midlife Map allows you to bring "big picture" perspective to your friends, as well as to yourself.

One of the things the Midlife Map does for you is to take the hundreds or thousands of components that could be relevant to the midlife struggle and reduces them to a few crystal-clear elements. There are two fundamental issues:

     (1) a person's dreams, and

     (2) emotional needs.

There are four "triggers" to midlife reevaluation:

     (1) disappointed dreams,

     (2) burnout,

     (3) aging, and

     (4) unmet emotional needs.

There are three stages in the midlife process:

     (1) midlife reevaluation,

     (2) midlife crisis, and

     (3) midlife crash/dropout.

Once you get the big picture, the whole midlife process becomes much more understandable, much more manageable, much more solvable.

Now that you have an overview of the Midlife Map (and the midlife process) I'd like to ask you, "Where are you in the process?" If you can see yourself at a given Map Point, you may even want to skip ahead in the book to that Map Point. Then read any other Map Points you feel will help you understand where you have been, where you are right now, or where to go from here.

Every person has three selves:

- We have a PUBLIC SELF that everyone sees;
- We have a PRIVATE SELF that only a close few have seen;
- We have a PERSONAL SELF that only we have ever seen. We've never told anyone else about it.

The personal self is what I think could accurately be referred to as our "heart." What's in a man's heart? A woman's heart? What's in *your* heart? Unlike books on mechanical engineering or airplane construction, how to cook the meal of the century, or how to get ahead in your career, this is a book of the heart. Reading this book honestly will require you to be extraordinarily candid with your own self. You can fool everyone else, but you can't fool yourself.

As you read through this book, I would encourage you to be true to who you are. If you feel more comfortable processing this material by yourself, wait until you've finished to discuss it with people. If you're the kind of person who needs to process things with other people, feel free to start now and share it with whomever you like.

My main concern is that you find a way to deal with your personal self and not just the public self that everyone sees. The "you" that's in front of the camera—or leading the group, the state, the corporation, the church—is probably not the self that is struggling inside with unfulfilled dreams or unmet needs. Neither is the private "you" that you discuss with your mate and your therapist and your family the real you. Find a way to get in touch with the real "you," which is your heart, the "you" that probably no one else has ever seen.

At the conclusion of each Map Point in this book, I will present you with a "Heart Probe." Sometimes it will be a chart for you to complete that will offer some insights. Sometimes it will be a checklist of personal behaviors or perspectives. Sometimes it will be a questionnaire. Sometimes it will simply be a single, profound question for you to think about.

In the "Heart Probe" I'll ask you to look deeply into your personal self. You don't have to report, defend, explain—just look deeply into your heart and be courageously honest with yourself. The "Heart Probe" will help you get in touch with your personal self, and help you make some decisions that move you toward a healthy, exciting, fulfilling life.

Are you ready for your first probe?

## Heart Probe:
As honestly as you can see yourself, where are you on the Midlife Map?

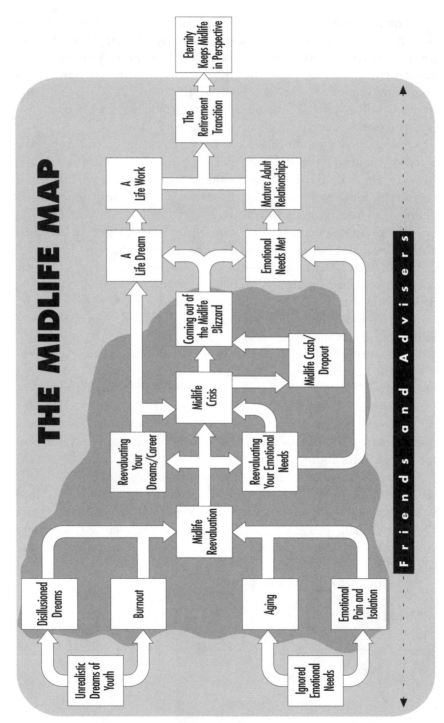

# THE MIDLIFE MAP

**Disillusioned Dreams**

**Unrealistic Dreams of Youth**

**Burnout**

**Midlife Reevaluation**

**Aging**

**Emotional Pain and Isolation**

**Ignored Emotional Needs**

**Reevaluating Your Dreams/Career**

**Reevaluating Your Emotional Needs**

**Midlife Crisis**

**Coming out of the Midlife Blizzard**

**Midlife Crash/Dropout**

**A Life Dream**

**A Life Work**

**Emotional Needs Met**

**The Retirement Transition**

**Mature Adult Relationships**

**Eternity Keeps Midlife in Perspective**

**Friends and Advisers**

© Bobb Biehl 1993

# Map Point 1: Friends and Advisers

*Identify and seek out the people who know you well and who can help you be objective about yourself.*

How often have you struggled with a given problem, wrestling with it over and over in your mind, unable to resolve it? Then a friend comes in and you tell him what you're struggling with and he says, "Oh, have you thought about ___?" and the problem is solved! Why? Because your friend was more objective about the situation than you were, though you had wrestled with the problem for hours. At the same time, there have probably been many times you have seen a friend struggling, and it's obvious to you what the situation or the problem or the answer is, simply because you're more objective about what she's dealing with than she is.

If I could reduce to a single word the primary value of the role played by spouse, friends, and mentors in the midlife process, it would have to be the word *objectivity*. Even though they are not as objective as a person who does not know you at all, or possibly a professional therapist might be, part of what they represent in the midlife discussion is objectivity.

## The Role Played by a Spouse: OBJECTIVITY

Some spouses are better equipped to deal with your midlife issues than others. Some find it easier to flex in the process than others. Some spouses don't want to discuss midlife issues at all; they don't want to hear your troubles. Some don't have—or take—the time to listen. Others are willing and eager to listen for hours on end. But if and when your mate *does* listen to you, he or she can provide a certain element of objectivity that is not available within the confines of your own thought process.

My wife, Cheryl, and I had a particular single friend we met for dinner on a regular basis over a period of time. We would discuss an issue, come to clarity, and the three of us would be in 100 percent agreement as to what the next step should be. The next week we'd get back together and our friend would be 90–180 degrees in a different direction altogether. Cheryl and I concluded that she and I discuss issues frequently enough that if my thinking begins to wander off track on a given issue, she is able to bring me back, and vice versa. We have a kind of balancing effect on each other in our marital relationship that a single person might not have. Ideally, if you are married, your spouse will be able to bring balance to your perspective.

If your spouse has never been through a midlife storm, it is possible there will be a judgmental attitude toward your confusion. If her head is clear, she may see no reason whatsoever for you to be in a blizzard of any kind. She may see your world very objectively, but have little empathy for what is going on in your mind and heart. It may seem to her as though you're walking around with a space helmet on. Inside the helmet, your private blizzard rages. She can see you clearly but believes you can't see anyone else as clearly. The reality of it is that she's probably right. Other people *can* see you more accurately than you can see them, but they can't experience the blizzard going on in your head and heart.

This is where spouses desperately need to realize that everyone is not alike. Just because they have not experienced the midlife blizzard doesn't mean that other people shouldn't or don't, or that they won't someday. For the moment, things are straight, orderly, and un-confused in their world. But they are unable to read what's going on inside your head where things may be quite different.

Sometimes, however, when you're in the middle of your midlife blizzard, your spouse may be in the middle of his or her own midlife blizzard, and you've got two people in a blizzard bumping into each other. The frustration mounts when both husband and wife are walking around in a blizzard state.

Another reality to consider is that occasionally when you hit the midlife years you also simultaneously become empty nesters. When the children leave home, often there's a period of six months to two years where the parents look at each other almost as strangers across the table. You've worked together on behalf of the children, but haven't related to each other directly for eighteen to twenty years. So a part of what you're trying to do in the midlife blizzard is to sort out your mate's approach to you, how she sees you, how objective she's able to be, how much you trust her counsel and wisdom and perspective.

If you are married, I'd like to ask you to check which of the following you feel best describes your mate at this point:

☐ 1. Objective and very helpful, flexible, able to process with me a great deal.

☐ 2. Not in a midlife blizzard, and sees no reason whatsoever that I should be. Considers the problem 100 percent mine.

☐ 3. Is in as much a blizzard as I am, going through his or her own midlife issues.

☐ 4. We are empty nesters married to strangers. We have to get to know each other at a whole new level.

Defining where your spouse is in the process is helpful in accepting him or her. It will also help when the time comes to communicate how you see the relationship and what you need from it.

## The Key Role Played by Friends: OBJECTIVITY

Friends are typically even more objective than mates. However, one of the main problems with friends is that when you're discussing your midlife blizzard, you may need days or weeks or months of processing to sort out all the pieces, and friends typically have only minutes or hours.

Another dimension of relating to friends about midlife issues is that your experience is like a "black box" to your friends. They cannot see inside your head and heart. Again, it's back to the space helmet analogy. They're sitting there talking to you, and they see your body as clearly as they can see anything. And they see this space helmet where your head should be, and inside is a blizzard through which they can't see your face. So a lot of times it's very difficult for them to know what to say and how to say it. They can see that you're in a blizzard, that you don't know how to get out of the blizzard, that you don't know how to get this space helmet off and let the snow just blow off somewhere. They simply do not know how to approach helping you.

Friends are often helpful in defining or refining a dream, and they can often be a part of the process of meeting your needs. But like your spouse, without some kind of objective road map to go by, they often feel intimidated by the prospect of discussing midlife issues with a person with a helmet full of snow. Especially if they haven't been through a similar storm.

This is where I would encourage you, if you have a close friend, to sit down together and go over the Midlife Map to evaluate where you are. Then, ask your friend to help you process very specifically how to get from where you are to where you want to go (the next Map Point).

## A Mentor's Role in Midlife: OBJECTIVITY

A mentor is more objective than a spouse, more personal than a therapist, and more committed than a "fair-weather friend." A mentor is constantly reevaluating, over time, the fundamental balance between your potential and your reality. In the book *Mentoring*, I define mentoring this way:

> *"Mentoring is a life-long relationship in which the mentor helps the protégé realize her or his God-given potential."*

One of the invaluable roles a mentor can play in your life is to help you move through situations like midlife blizzards, taking the time and energy and, if necessary, resources to help you through the process. Another role the mentor plays is to help you adjust your dreams to reality, when necessary. When it becomes obvious to the mentor that you will never be an all-pro player, and you'll never even make the pro team, he needs to sit down with you and help you process that reality, as compared to simply ignoring it, like many friends would. The role of the mentor is to help you see where you are and help you know how to get to your full potential over a lifetime.

Here again, as I suggested with the spouse and friends, sit down with your mentor and show him or her the Midlife Map, and say, "Here's where I am today. Here's how I think I got here. Could you help me get to the next Map Point?" For example, if you're at Map Point 8 (Midlife Reevaluation), then ask your mentor to help you think through your career options and to understand how to get your emotional needs met. If you're at Map Point 11 (Midlife Crisis), ask him or her to help you understand how to move to Map Point 13 (Coming Out of the Midlife Blizzard) and begin to come out of the midlife blizzard.

I have been assuming that you have at least one mentor, if not two or three. If you have no mentor at all, you might want to consider reading my book *Mentoring: Confidence in Finding a Mentor and Becoming One*. An effective mentor is an extraordinarily helpful person in the process of weathering your midlife storm.

In summary, the role that spouses, friends, and mentors play in your life is to provide you with a constant sense of objectivity (to the best of their ability). Ideally, they will also provide continuing love and care and encouragement that things will get better. It's important that you realize that many friends are there to help. They really want to help you in this midlife confusion, but they simply don't know how. They don't have an objective process to take you through. They don't know which of the thousand questions you ask them are the most relevant ones.

Sit down with your spouse, with a friend, a mentor, or a counselor, and go over the Midlife Map and communicate with them where you've been, where you are, and what help you need in getting to the very next Map Point. Focus on those issues critical to taking the next step, rather than all the hundreds of questions floating around inside your head.

---

## Heart Probe:

Who really understands me?

Who do I really trust to give me wise counsel and perspective?

---

Remember: spouses, friends, and mentors are often the best people to help you redefine your dreams and to meet the needs of your heart.

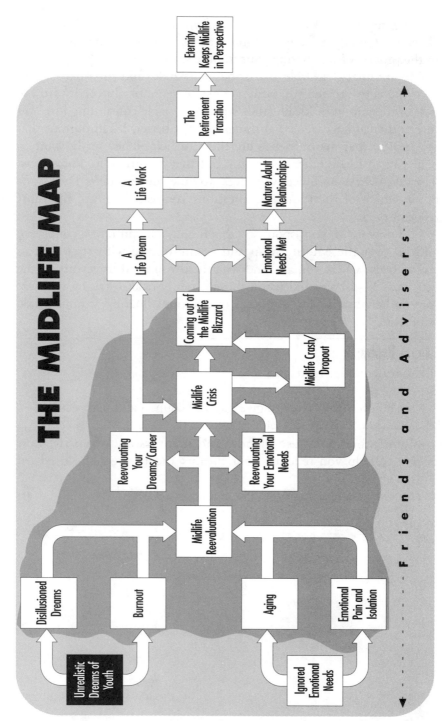

# THE MIDLIFE MAP

Unrealistic Dreams of Youth

Disillusioned Dreams

Burnout

Aging

Emotional Pain and Isolation

Ignored Emotional Needs

Midlife Reevaluation

Reevaluating Your Dreams/Career

Reevaluating Your Emotional Needs

Midlife Crisis

Midlife Crash/Dropout

Coming out of the Midlife Blizzard

A Life Dream

A Life Work

Emotional Needs Met

Mature Adult Relationships

The Retirement Transition

Eternity Keeps Midlife in Perspective

- - - - - - Friends and Advisers - - - - - -

© Bobb Biehl 1993

# Map Point 2: Unrealistic Dreams of Youth

*Prior to midlife we have energizing and inspirational dreams. Many of these dreams are illusions based on an inaccurate self-assessment. But unrealistic as these dreams may be, they are still very energizing.*

Remember when you were a child, or perhaps a teen, or maybe even in your twenties, and you had a grand and glorious dream of what your life would be like some day? You had dreams of what you were going to accomplish, the role you were going to play, the destiny you were going to fulfill. Remember how energizing that felt? How electric it became whenever you had the chance to get away and dream your dream again?

Dreams provide energy. Even if it is not accurate, or viable, or realistic—even if it is 100 percent illusion—a dream gives vigor in the younger years. It makes a person feel strong and alive.

## Some Dreams Are Very Naive

Some dreams are little more than illusions based on lack of accurate self-perception. In youth there seems to be an unlimited amount of time, energy, and money. Therefore, anything is possible.

Often the dreams we have as children are actually the dreams of our parents, the fantasies that they had for their own lives which went unfulfilled. An example is the person who wants to be a doctor because a parent said, "My son someday is going to grow up and be a doctor!" The child's response twenty years—$200,000 in medical school bills—later is, "It's not me!"

Another reality is that many times as young adults we announce dreams and "commit ourselves publicly," only to realize later that those dreams were unrealistic, naive, and could never become reality. It's embarrassing to downsize one's dreams. It's also frustrating to have other people around us who dream for us—bigger than our own dreams. Bigger even than our ability to accomplish those dreams. But we have the dreams, nonetheless. As young dreamers we dream of what might be, what someday we will do, be, have, who we'll help. And such dreams provide enormous amounts of energy in those young years.

If, however, there is a single word that could most accurately describe these young dreams, it would be the word *naive*. We do not have an accurate self-perception—an understanding of who we are— in our teens or early twenties. We simply guess at who we are and try to become what we think we might be. But to have an accurate, adult perception of who we are is beyond us. So we launch our dreams without paying any heed to the realities we eventually meet up with in our late thirties and early forties.

## A Perspective on Young Dreams by Decade

*The First Decade Dreams: Age 1 to 10—Parents*
The dreams that most shape us as children are the dreams of our parents. The dream of "my son/daughter, the doctor." The dreams of children are primarily to please and/or to protect their parents someday, such as the poor child who dreams of making it out of the squalor and hunger of early life.

*Teen Dreams: Age 11 to 20—Peers*
Teenaged dreams are typically designed to impress peers. The typical teen focus is no longer on impressing or pleasing parents, but rather on what would gain respect or position among peers. Our teen dreams are idealistic dreams based on a romantic view of the world and without an adequate understanding of the realities either within ourselves or in the world. But often these dreams too last into adulthood. There are many accounts of dreams formed in the teenage years that have lasted for an entire lifetime. But a high percentage of teenage dreams that I've encountered turned out to be an illusion, based on adult realities. (see Map Point 4 [Disillusioned Dreams])

*Twenties Dreams: Age 21 to 30—Profession*
The dreams in our twenties are more realistic but are still somewhat

naive, and they are primarily not oriented to parents or to peers but to our profession. What will I someday be in my profession, my career, my work? What could I someday do that would lead to great acclaim, make a significant difference, lead to security, income, possessions, respect?

In this stage of life we're still inexperienced enough to be basing a lot of our dreams on very faulty assumptions in terms of who we are, what we're really capable of, and what the real needs are, as well as what the realistic solutions are. And frequently dreams developed in the twenties become disillusionments early in the midlife years. But some of the dreams developed in the twenties last—with the help of mentors, friends, a supportive spouse—into adulthood and become real over time.

## Objective Self-Assessment Is Critical but Often Lacking

What a young dreamer really needs is objective assessment from friends and mentors. Not excessively positive or negative assessments, but *objective* assessments that can help him or her see strengths, areas of struggle, and the realities from a more adult perspective.

If a person is wise and fortunate in their early thirties, they gather a trusted personal "advisory council"—a group of two to five people— around them who can be a continual source of objective feedback and input. These are people who can say, "Here's how I see you; here are your strengths; I think you could really do this; I think that's a little bit heavy right now; I think that's terribly unrealistic, but if you want to try it, go for it; just don't be discouraged if you don't succeed the first year." These objective, supportive, encouraging comments are extraordinarily helpful—especially in the younger years.

The following are ten questions that would be helpful for you to ask your closest friends or advisory council every so often:

☐ 1. What do you see as my single greatest strength?
☐ 2. What am I really good at that has surprised you recently?
☐ 3. What do you think are the blind sides I should be aware of?
☐ 4. What areas would you encourage me to grow in to get ready for the future?
☐ 5. Where do you see me ten years from now?
☐ 6. What do you think should be the top three priorities I should work on this coming year?
☐ 7.What person or persons do you think I should meet at

this point in my life?

☐  8.  What cautions do you have for me at this point in my life?

☐  9.  What potentials do you see in me that you think I don't see in me?

☐ 10.  If you were me, what would you be thinking about right now?

Asking close friends questions like these every year or so narrows the distance between your dreams and reality, so it squeezes a lot of the illusion out of the dreams later on. It helps you to be a realistic dreamer. Never stop dreaming, but as a young dreamer you need to be working toward getting your dreams to line up with reality, to burst the illusions that later end in disillusionment.

WARNING: You can get all the advice and counsel and input from close friends and advisers and mentors that you want, but the reality is that you need to see all input as advice that helps you decide what you're going to do with your life. No other person should have the position in your life of telling you what to do as an adult. Other people are advisers in your life, not deciders. The responsibility for making the final decision rests squarely on your shoulders, and you live with the consequences, both positive and negative. Leave no room to look back and blame someone else for having told you the wrong thing. Advice, counsel, and perspective add dimension to how you see yourself. They help you see things which otherwise you may not see or understand. But, in the final analysis, it's up to you to define dreams that are based on reality, not on illusion—that are mature, and not naive.

---

## Heart Probe:

How would you define your dreams from age one to ten?

How would you define your teenage dreams?

How would you define your dreams in your twenties?

Who are the objective people you've counted on to be your sounding board, to keep your dreams in line with reality over the years?

---

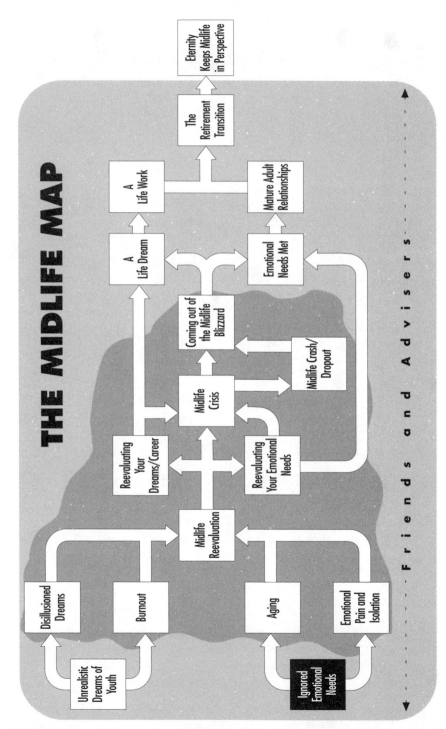

THE MIDLIFE MAP

Eternity Keeps Midlife in Perspective

The Retirement Transition

A Life Work

A Life Dream

Coming out of the Midlife Blizzard

Midlife Crisis

Reevaluating Your Dreams/Career

Midlife Reevaluation

Reevaluating Your Emotional Needs

Midlife Crash/Dropout

Emotional Needs Met

Mature Adult Relationships

Disillusioned Dreams

Burnout

Unrealistic Dreams of Youth

Aging

Emotional Pain and Isolation

Ignored Emotional Needs

- - - - Friends and Advisers - - - -

© Bobb Biehl 1993

# Map Point 3: Ignored Emotional Needs

*Prior to midlife we have unmet emotional needs which we tend to ignore in the process of surviving and succeeding in our careers.*

Unmet emotional needs are like time bombs ticking their way to destructive explosions in midlife years. The problem is that most people, prior to reaching midlife, are so committed to survival and then success in their business or other career that they take very little time to stop and reflect on questions such as *What are my needs? How are my needs being met? What would I have to change in my own life to get those needs met?*

A large part of the reason people don't stop to look at unmet needs in a very definitive way is they simply do not have the framework to decide what their needs really are. As a matter of fact, I think that most people assume that they have 50 needs—or 100, or 300, or 1,000 needs! How is it possible to decide which needs to meet? You may feel like you have so many needs you couldn't possibly get it down to a realistic, achievable list.

There are actually *only eight basic needs* (discussed in detail in my book *Why You Do What You Do*) that are the common denominators in all people. Essentially, people do what they do for these eight reasons:

- To be loved
- To make a significant difference
- To be admired
- To be recognized
- To be appreciated

- To be secure
- To be respected
- To be accepted

## Masks Make True Intimacy Impossible

Recall for just a moment the three selves every person has: the public self that everyone sees, the private self that only close friends and relatives see in private, and then the personal self that only you have ever seen. When a person puts on a mask in public (e.g., a jock, a professor, a singer) and hides behind it and relates to everyone he knows based on that persona, intimacy becomes very difficult, if not impossible. Most conversations will happen at a mask-to-mask level, focusing on occupation, activities, possessions.

Some conversations happen at a private level. These are the discussions you have with your spouse, your children, your close friends, your buddies, about people, about insights into people.

But intimacy (allowing another person a glimpse of your personal self) is difficult to achieve wearing a mask. With your mask on, others are unaware of the needs you have, and as a result no one is meeting those needs.

A lot of times wives say, "We don't have an intimate relationship." The husband turns and says, "What in the world does she mean by that? We have sex a lot!"

While physical intimacy can occur when you grant another person access to your body, emotional intimacy is when you let another person go beyond your mask and beyond even what close friends and family see, and let them see a part of your heart that you've never opened up to anyone else. A true heart-to-heart conversation is where one person shares things they've never told anyone, and the other person responds at the same level. It's at this level of intimacy that you can share with a person, "I really need love, significance, admiration, recognition, appreciation, security, respect, acceptance. But of all those, the number one thing I need is _____."

Often it takes people thirty to forty years to have enough emotional pain inside their hearts to be willing to risk taking off the mask and telling someone else how they really feel and what they really need. However, unless there is an environment of unconditional love, the mask never comes off, the barriers never come down, and the person simply keeps unmet needs growing in the heart, and the time bomb keeps ticking its way to a destructive explosion in the midlife years.

## The Pace of Life Often Covers Felt Needs

Living in survival stage (typically the twenties) you wonder, *Am I going to be able to pay the bills? Am I going to be able to keep this job? Am I going to be able to support my family?* etc. By the thirties, your questions are probably more along the lines of, *How big can the company get? How high can I go in the company? How much money can I make? Should we buy another condominium?* etc. But with all the energy it takes to survive and succeed, often our emotional needs remain totally unaddressed.

I remember talking to someone from Gary, Indiana, and I said, "How do you stand the smell of those steel mills every day?" His response: "It smells like money to me!" The point, obviously, is that he was ignoring his own health risks, his own discomfort in order to survive and/or succeed.

Another "cure-all" in the early twenties is the myth that "enough sex cures anything!" When we need love, admiration, appreciation, security, respect, or acceptance, we turn to sex. Somehow, we assume that sex is close enough to love, admiration, appreciation, security, respect, or acceptance. But as we grow older and enter the midlife years, we begin to understand that not all sex is love, not all sex involves respect, and not all sex includes acceptance. Progressively we realize that we have needs that have never been—and can never be—addressed simply by having sex with our mate.

It's also amazing how many people have assumed that super success would ultimately meet all of their unmet needs. This is a fantasy that leads to a lot of disillusionment in the midlife years. But in our late twenties and early thirties, we sort of assume that if we had enough money, if we could reach all of our goals, then surely our unmet emotional needs would be no problem at all. Probably one of the most insightful bumper stickers making its way down some freeway tonight is the one which says, "Money only solves money problems!"

Prior to our midlife years we are surviving, succeeding, and ignoring. Ignoring the emotional needs that we have had hidden deep in our heart since childhood. And when those needs are ignored and we don't find new and better and improved ways of relating to people to have those needs met, they become a time bomb waiting to go off in the midlife years.

## Heart Probe:

What are your unmet emotional needs?

As you rate the eight needs listed earlier in the chapter which is your number one need? What do you need more than anything else?

Does your mate know what you need from him or her?

Do confidants, intimate friends know what you need from them?

Does your mentor know what you need from her/him?

Who knows what you need, besides yourself? If you haven't told them, chances are they aren't going to figure it out.

I've asked many couples, married thirty years, "What is your spouse's greatest emotional need?" Neither partner had a clue. This sets both up for severe pain in the midlife years and leaves both vulnerable to the temptation of an affair. First, identify your own unmet emotional needs, and then identify your mate's unmet emotional needs. Then set out to learn new and improved ways of meeting those needs before you hit the midlife years.

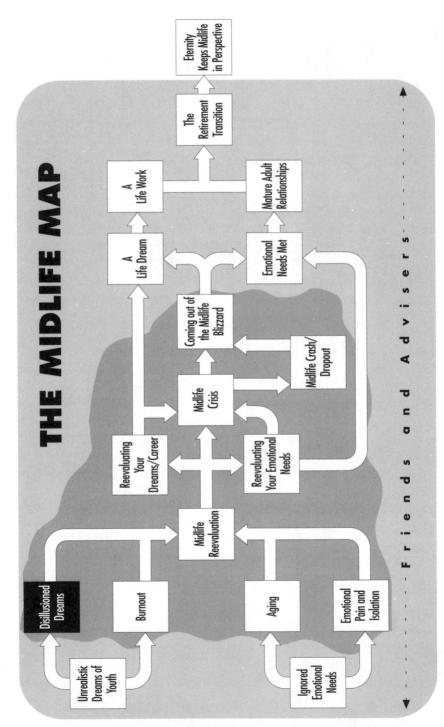

# THE MIDLIFE MAP

Eternity Keeps Midlife in Perspective

The Retirement Transition

A Life Work

A Life Dream

Mature Adult Relationships

Coming out of the Midlife Blizzard

Emotional Needs Met

Midlife Crisis

Reevaluating Your Dreams/Career

Midlife Crash/Dropout

Reevaluating Your Emotional Needs

Midlife Reevaluation

Disillusioned Dreams

Burnout

Aging

Emotional Pain and Isolation

Unrealistic Dreams of Youth

Ignored Emotional Needs

- - - - - Friends and Advisers - - - - -

© Bobb Biehl 1993

# Map Point 4: Disillusioned Dreams: The First Midlife Reevaluation "Trigger"

*In our late thirties to early forties—depending on who we are and how quickly we meet the midlife blizzard—the dream disillusionment process begins.*

There is no disillusionment unless there is first an illusion.

Prior to the midlife blizzard, life often seems to be going along acceptably. You have a young dream, based on illusion in many cases, but still a dream. You have unmet needs that are ignored in the survival and success stages—unmet, but they don't seem all that pressing. When the midlife blizzard begins, there are four "triggers" that can happen almost simultaneously—realizations that trigger the midlife reevaluation process:

1. the disillusionment of dreams (Map Point 4);
2. burnout (Map Point 5);
3. the aging process (Map Point 6); and
4. unmet emotional needs (Map Point 7).

I'm starting with the disillusionment of dreams even though any of the four triggers may actually occur first in a given person's life. All four are typically involved in creating and starting the serious midlife reevaluation.

Dreams, even fantasy dreams, are energizing. You think of what will be someday, and receive tremendous power to face today, tomorrow, and the next day. But when you begin to realize that your dream of someday will never be a reality, there is a sadness of heart that is indescribable to the nondreamer. With a dream you have a north star, an orientation point. No matter how discouraged you get, no matter how tired, you look to the dream and there's something to get out of bed for in the morning, something to keep going toward—a championship to win, a presidency to gain, an election to win. But when the young dreams begin to die, it's as if the north star goes out. There is not only a disheartening sense of disillusionment but a "dark night" disorientation as well.

Sometimes the dream dies quickly. Sometimes it dies over a period of years. But when the dream dies, it is typically not with a huge clap of thunder, but with a gentle, quiet sound like the bursting of a soap bubble in a child's backyard. The neighbors probably won't hear it; often it doesn't make a sound loud enough for spouse or children to hear it, or even close friends. It is simply a "poof" deep in the recesses of our hearts, where we realize that the dream we have carried for so many years is, in fact, an illusion and not a reality.

Whenever you reach the point in life where you have been disillusioned by something, it is very important to realize that prior to being disillusioned, there had to be an illusion. Making a list of your disillusionments (and therefore your illusions) might be a very helpful exercise if this is where you are on the Midlife Map at the moment.

Sometimes you're disillusioned with someone else's dream. Perhaps you work for someone who tells you that your company will be the best, that your team will make it to the finals, that you or your candidate will be elected. And then the illusion bursts like a soap bubble when your team leader comes to you and says, "Not only will we not get the brass ring, but our contract has not been renewed and we're all out of a job."

Sometimes the illusion is your dream to grow old with your mate. Then, unexpectedly, your mate leaves you, and the painful disillusionment is that your mate is not the person you thought he or she was.

All of these disillusionments begin to trigger a midlife reevaluation. Questions come such as *In what can I trust? What's real, what's unreal? Where am I going from here?* And these simple, yet profound questions begin to fly around in your brain and heart, and the future begins to get a little bit blurred. And the more you think about them, the harder you think about them, the more they splinter off into other "sub-questions." *What will I do about the house? Where will I go? Will I ever get a good job again? Do I still have potential? Is my confidence still there? Do I really have what it takes?*

These questions may be unanswerable at a given point, but as your mind begins to fill with literally hundreds of them, a mental and emotional blur is created.

## When Reality Threatens to Destroy Your Dreams

When a dream is finally abandoned, broken, ended, it feels like pulling the plug that lights a lamp out of the wall. There is a drastic reduction in energy. Without the energy of a dream there is very little that pulls you out of bed in the morning. And as you begin to feel the aging process, you may wonder, *Is it just because I'm getting older that I don't have the energy to get up and go, the zip I used to have, or is it because of the lost dream?* Often it's a combination that's not always easy to sort out.

Some dreams *should* be killed. An uncle giving his unwanted advice has said for years, "that's not realistic, you'll never be governor, you'll never be head coach, you'll never get the job, you'll never make a million dollars, that's the wrong business for you," etc., and perhaps you have been trying for years to prove him wrong. Whenever someone else tries to kill our dream, it simply adds internal fire to prove him wrong. But sometimes it is the better part of wisdom to simply "eat crow" and move on! It is typically far less painful when we kill a dream ourselves. To say, "Regardless of what Uncle Zingo did or didn't say, this dream is now dead. It's time to move on to something else."

To help you spot what may have been a dream that died within you, here is a list of just a few of the dreams that I've seen bring this disillusionment to people:

*"I Don't Think I'll Ever Be President" (political blockage)*
When you realize for the first time that you will never reach the level in the company that you had originally planned, it can be devastating. It creates literally hundreds of questions: *Should I stay in the company? Should I go somewhere else? Have I got what it takes? Was I a good leader in the first place?* etc.

*"I'm Not Presidential" (lack of ability)*
Though similar to the first example, this is not about opportunity. This statement of disillusion is based on the conclusion that you don't have what it takes to be the president. The dream that has been your north star for years ends up like someone turning out a light, and you ask yourself, *Should I go to a smaller company where I could be president? Should I just live with being a vice president?* and so on.

45

*"I Used to Be President" (failure or misfortune)*

The organizational pyramid is very small at the top and only a few people ever become president. But there are people who do achieve that office and then lose it. In my career I've dealt with many such men and women who found it extremely difficult to regain a dream or believe in it or trust the system. Once you've been relieved later in life, once you've been fired, it's very, very difficult to believe in the presidential dream again. And that triggers a whole series of questions such as: *Do I really want to be president? Should I retire early? Should I just go off and start my own company?* And such questions may begin to blur your vision for the future.

Sometimes the failure of a person in the presidency has nothing to do with their own ability, but is a response to the economy. I had a client who had a very successful real estate development company. The economy dropped, and for about ten years he struggled to pay off debtors while trying to find a new niche for himself in the real estate development arena. For a number of years there were literally thousands of self-doubt questions that blurred his thinking.

And then there's the trauma that comes with never getting the big break, the record-setting sale that never comes. Many people dream forever of selling a million-dollar policy, of selling a big unit of some kind, believing that once they make the big score, things will be just fine. And the reality finally dawns on them that *I'll never make the big sale, I'll never make the big leagues, and my dream is an illusion.*

Many people do not have lofty dreams of the big sale, the governorship, becoming company president. But the one voted most likely to succeed, who doesn't, has an even longer drop to the bottom of reality. Many people who thought they would be millionaires by thirty-five are still in debt. And when they get to thirty-five or forty, the dreams of the presidency, the dreams of the big sale, of being a millionaire, of being next in line, begin to fade and fail. And when that happens, the energy that comes from that dream begins to dampen. In the end, you have all the responsibilities of making a living day-to-day, but there is no motivation to keep jumping out of bed in the morning.

We've been talking, so far, about the professional dreams. But there are also personal dreams. Many times these dreams die in the late thirties. Sometimes parents get divorced and the dream of having perfect parents and a "Leave It to Beaver" family are shattered.

Sometimes the dream is that your children are going to be pro athletes, and they don't even make the high school team. To a parent who has invested hundreds, even thousands of hours helping the child become an athlete, this is very disillusioning, very discouraging. Sometimes it's a mate who leaves saying, "I don't love you anymore."

Sometimes the disillusionment is of a physical nature. Dr. Ken Martin is a world-class orthopedic surgeon in Little Rock, Arkansas. Dr. Martin is the founder of the Martin Sports Clinic. He does a lot of surgeries on some of the finest athletes of the region. One day as we were driving together he said, "Do you know what the hardest part of being a surgeon is for me?" I had no real idea. "It is telling a thirty-eight-year-old athlete, whose sense of self-worth has come from his physical prowess for thirty years, that his athletic days are over."

Occasionally the death of a dream starts with the accidental, or premature death of a close friend. A buddy dies, a mentor dies, and there's a disillusionment with life. There is an assumption that life should go on and on with that buddy, that friend, and you should grow old together. When a friend dies there is often a dramatic disillusionment and anger, a sense of dark gray grief in your mind and heart. It creates a small blizzard of questions about God, life, the worth of anything, the meaning of anything.

The bottom line is that it is very difficult to maintain a zest for living, an energy, an excitement about life, when our dream bubble bursts. It sends us into a period of questioning that in one fell swoop leaves our head full of blowing snowlike questions, creating blurred vision, and our north star is no longer there. Life seems suddenly a lot less predictable than before. With very little energy and a lot of questions floating around in our minds and hearts, the midlife reevaluation process is triggered.

## Confidence Is a By-Product of Predictability

When people first hear me say that "confidence is a by-product of predictability," I get a lot of blank stares. You may have some questions too, so let me explain this principle with a "what if."

What if :
- you are a marathon runner;
- you have won every race you have run for the past three years;
- you feel 100 percent healthy; and

47

- your knees have never given you any trouble; they are predictable.

You run with confidence!

What if:

- this marathon your knee pops out at mile marker eighteen;
- you go sprawling into the cinders; and
- your knee is in a brace for the next 3 months.

Your knee is suddenly not as predictable, so you run with less confidence. But you train hard, and a year later your are ready to race again. Your running confidence returns to 99 percent of your old confidence level before the accident.

What if:

- you start your first marathon after the accident feeling great;
- on mile marker ten your knee goes again—into the cinders.

You will never again run with the same degree of confidence. You have knees with limited predictability. Therefore, you have limited running confidence. Confidence is a by-product of predictability!

When your dreams break, when disillusions come, when the dream's no longer a dream but a memory, it triggers three fundamental things:

(1) A drastic reduction of the energy which comes from having a dream;

(2) An enormous number of questions that begin to swirl in your mind; and

(3) A blurred vision for the future, which makes it seem very unpredictable.

As a result of this unpredictability, your confidence begins to wobble and droop, perhaps for the very first time in your adult life. The thing to remember is that this disillusionment is temporary. It feels at times as though it is permanent and will never again be remedied. But given a few months or years, you will find a new dream. And it is possible to find new dreams that are based much more on reality and an accurate self-perception, which will again replace the energy, reduce the number of questions, and restore the predictability and, therefore, the confidence. But at the time of the disillusionment, it is extraordinarily difficult to pick yourself up and get yourself back on track. That's why I refer to it as one of the triggers of the midlife reevaluation process.

One of the other things you need to keep in mind at this point is that you may have kept your dream very much in your heart. The people around you may not understand how much the lost dream meant to you. Even if they did, they may not realize that it's gone, they may not realize the mental and emotional adjustments you've made to come to terms with letting it go. So they may still assume you have the same energy, focus, and direction that you felt when the dream was still alive.

As a result, they may expect you to be up, confident, and enthusiastic, when in fact, you are down, insecure, and confused. The difference between what you are and what they expect you to be is a real mystery to them. It is only as you are able to share with them how devastating the disillusionment or the death of that dream is, that they can even begin to comprehend the struggle of your heart and mind at this moment.

But as devastating as the death of a dream is, it is simply one of four things that come together in sort of a convergent "downer" to catalyze the midlife reevaluation process.

---

## Heart Probe:

In your heart of hearts, what is the dream that is now on its last gasping breath or has died?

Make a list of all the questions that the death of that dream has created in your heart. Get them out of your mind and onto paper.

How much energy loss have you felt due to the death of the dream? How hard is it for you to get up and get going in the morning, compared to how you felt when you still believed in the dream?

You are now beginning to be able to assess just how devastating the death of your dream has been in your heart and mind and why it is so powerful in creating some of the midlife blizzard and triggering the whole reevaluation process.

You may also find it helpful to make a list of your disillusionments (and therefore your illusions).

**Disillusion**                                    **Illusion**

---

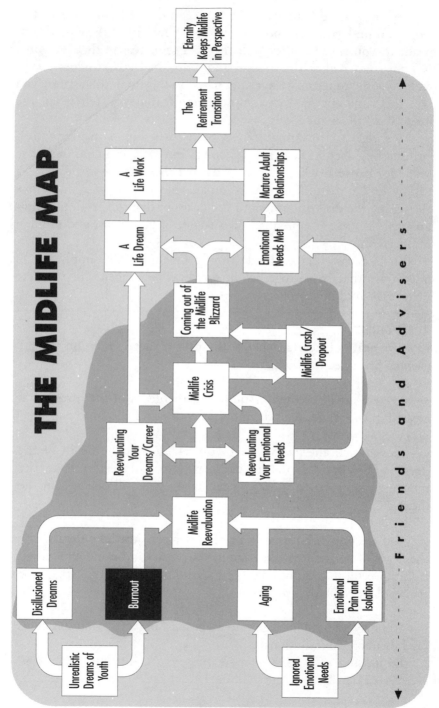

# THE MIDLIFE MAP

Eternity Keeps Midlife in Perspective

The Retirement Transition

A Life Work

A Life Dream

Coming out of the Midlife Blizzard

Midlife Crisis

Midlife Crash/ Dropout

Mature Adult Relationships

Emotional Needs Met

Reevaluating Your Dreams/Career

Reevaluating Your Emotional Needs

Midlife Reevaluation

Disillusioned Dreams

Burnout

Unrealistic Dreams of Youth

Aging

Emotional Pain and Isolation

Ignored Emotional Needs

- - - - - - - Friends and Advisers - - - - - - - -

© Bobb Biehl 1993

# Map Point 5: Burnout: The Second Midlife Reevaluation "Trigger"

*When we try so hard, for so long, to reach certain dreams that we can't seem to achieve, our natural energy gets exhausted.*

"Fatigue makes cowards of us all," according to Vince Lombardi, the legendary coach of the Green Bay Packers. And, it turns us introspective and negative. Whenever you get fatigued, tired, exhausted, you begin to question yourself, your own abilities, whether or not you'll ever "make it." And you begin to respond to your own questions with negative answers. Unrealistically negative answers.

## Burnout Makes Dreams Seem 100 Percent Unattainable!

As though the death of a dream wasn't enough, add to that a deep state of fatigue—burnout. When you've got thousands of questions swirling around in your mind and heart and no energy to pursue them, pretty soon you're working about 99 percent on *drive energy*—trying to make enough money to pay the bills or keep life going on an even keel. But you don't have the *natural energy*, so you begin burning up your reserves, living on adrenaline. Sooner or later, the natural reserve is gone and even the adrenaline energy is gone, and you end up in a state of utter fatigue, or burnout.

When you are in the middle of a burnout kind of situation, dreams seem 100 percent unattainable. Even if you have alternative dreams in different directions, your confidence and interest in pursuing them are nearly zero when you're in such a state.

# Role Preference Inventory: Predictable Burnout Points

A very common unspoken assumption in the minds of most people seems to be, "Everyone is basically like me—or they will be when they grow up!" It is important to see differences as complimentary strengths, not as immaturities. One of the most dependable tools available to help a person see how you, I, and the next person are fundamentally different is a simple inventory known as the Role Preference Inventory.

In 1973, I was working full time on the executive team of World Vision International, a nonprofit humanitarian organization. Today, they care for hundreds of thousands of needy children around the world. My assignment, at the time, was the directing of the volunteer program. While there, I designed and developed a little money container in the shape of a loaf of bread with a fish symbol embossed in the top. We called it the "Love Loaf." Your church may have had the program. You may have seen a Love Loaf at a checkout counter in a restaurant or other place of business. You may even have had one on your meal table. World Vision now has over 6,000 volunteers who service the Love Loaf in business establishments. Since its establishment, the Love Loaf program has raised tens of millions of dollars to help feed hungry people around the world.

In the process of developing the Love Loaf program, I concluded that over a period of the next fifty years or so, I would likely be involved in originating and developing hundreds of ideas. Therefore, it would be wise for me to "mark my trail" and keep track of the stages each and every idea goes through as it develops.

One day my assistant, Patty Lewis, approached me in a state of rather obvious frustration. "When are you ever going to let this program settle down and become routine?"

Her question actually shocked me, as I had never once considered such a strange idea. My immediate response was "The day I die or the day I leave the program is probably the first day it will become routine."

I was about thirty-two years old at the time, and as embarrassing as it is to admit today, this was the first time it ever dawned on me that everyone was not like me! After that encounter it was as though I had a brand-new pair of eyeglasses to see how people really differ. I began to see that I really enjoyed the design and the development phases of a program or project. But, when it got into the maintenance stage, I was totally bored. The settled-down maintenance stage was exactly where Patty began to get comfortable with it.

Over time it has become crystal clear that there are very specific, predictable differences in the phase of a project's development that different people enjoy. And it is easy to predict team chemistry based on a person's preferences. Through years of observations and refinements, I now believe that there are five very basic phases through which each and every idea must eventually pass to reach its full potential. Every person you know prefers one of the phases more than the other four. These phases are mutually exclusive by definition.

### 1. The Design Phase

The Designer is a person who prefers discussing and understanding the theoretical design of anything. He/she prefers solving theoretical problems with original theoretical solutions but doesn't enjoy the practical process of creating a prototype. Once the problem is solved theoretically, the burnout clock starts ticking almost immediately. Designers tend to be problem-oriented. But the problems are theoretical problems, not problems of a practical nature.

### 2. The Design/Development Phase

The Designer/Developer is a person who prefers to take on a tough cause, mission, or dream and to set clear, strategic, long-range goals. He/she prefers to define the problems, come up with original solutions, and develop a working prototype. However, near the end of the development of the prototype he/she predictably hits what I have come to call "the 7/8ths wall" and begin to lose interest at a very rapid rate. Burnout is a real danger at this point.

Designer/Developers are as close to enjoying both goals and problems as anyone. They tend to be goal-oriented, but acutely problem-aware.

### 3. The Development Phase

The Developer is a person who prefers to be given clear and challenging goals and one to three working models, or examples, and adapt the best from each to create a new model that is an improvement over any of the existing models. But, when the goal has been reached (or two years and one day has elapsed!), fatigue sets in.

Developers tend to be the very most goal-oriented. They rarely enjoy the process of dealing with problems.

*4. The Development/Maintenance Phase*
The Developer/Maintainer is a person who prefers to take an existing system, organization, or project and solve the practical systems problems, refine, debug, and improve it to the point where it is running smoothly, and the results are even better than expected. But, when things begin running too smoothly (perhaps four or five years into a project's history) the Developer/Maintainer wants a bit more challenge.

Developer/Maintainers tend to be clearly problem-oriented. But these are not the designer's theoretical problems. Rather, these are very down-to-earth, practical, system problems. Rarely do Developer/Maintainers enjoy setting and/or being held accountable to reach goals.

*5. The Maintenance Phase*
The Maintainer prefers to be given a responsibility where the policies, procedures, and systems are well-defined. The symptoms of burnout may not show up for twenty or thirty years for a Maintainer. Disloyalty on the part of a team member, however, can often lead to early burnout for a Maintainer, and the desire for a change.

Maintainers are definitely problem-oriented. But, they are actually oriented to problem prevention. Though they are oriented by problems, Maintainers dislike problems, and see them as very disruptive.

Shortly after this insight, another revelation hit me like the proverbial "ton of bricks"! I was working with my father, who was night auditor at Shanty Creek Lodge, a world-class ski resort and golf course in Bellaire, Michigan. Since I was then living in California and didn't get to see Dad very often, I would go to work with him (all night) and chat and snack with him on his breaks.

One night he said that what he really wanted in a job was to:
1. to be given a very specific assignment;
2. to manage (lead) no one;
3. to be paid a fair wage.

That was the very first time in my life that it occurred to me that not everyone wants to be the captain of everything he is in. At the time, I fully assumed that sooner or later I would become the president of whatever I was a part of. I truly—and naively—assumed that everyone else really wanted the same thing. It finally dawned on me that some fully mature adults preferred to be what today I call "strong players," some prefer to be "presidential captains," and others prefer to be "middle captains."

These are the three levels of leadership for each of the five developmental phases listed above:

1. Presidential Captain

   The president, the head coach, the senior pastor. The one who wants to be "where the buck stops," to be the "go to" person, to be fully in charge.

2. Middle Captain

   The vice president, the assistant coach, the associate pastor. Middle Captains want to lead a team—their own team. Leading brings them great pleasure. But under pressure, they prefer having a leader make the final decisions.

3. Strong Player

   The person who enjoys playing the game, maybe even being the superstar, wants their input to be respected, but does not want to be the captain of anything, especially under pressure!

## The Role Preference Grid

(Note: Role Preference is used by special permission from Masterplanning Group from its copyrighted resource, the "Role Preference Inventory.")

| | Designer | Designer - Developer | Developer | Developer - Maintainer | Maintainer |
|---|---|---|---|---|---|
| Presidential Captain | | | | | |
| Middle Captain | | | | | |
| Strong Player | | | | | |

It is my experience that everyone who wants to be a part of any team prefers one of the above fifteen boxes. When I know a person's preference, it is easy to predict their team—and personal—chemistry with the people in each of the other fourteen boxes.

The level a person prefers is not correlated to their interest in goal-setting or problem-solving. Some people at all levels prefer goal-setting and others at all levels prefer problem-solving.

I have frequently asked the senior executive of an organization to guess what those reporting directly to her/him would state as their role preferences. Then, by first names only, I begin to explain the team chemistry of the people who report to her/him. It is easy to go for thirty–sixty minutes knowing only first names (not age, race, position, company history, etc.) and rarely miss predicting what the natural chemistry is between people on the staff.

Following are but a few of the wide variety of predictable factors, based on your Role Preference:

- Values
- Enjoyment
- Orientation
- Creativity
- Burnout point
- Problem/goal-orientation

Below is a grid showing a few of the many things which are predictable based on the phase you prefer, and it can help you "see behind the smile" of the person you are interviewing or who is on your staff. As you will see by the very last row, the Role Preference Inventory can also help you predict how each of your staff members looks at burnout.

| Phase | 1. Design | 2. Design Develop | 3. Develop | 4. Develop Maintain | 5. Maintain |
|---|---|---|---|---|---|
| High Value —likes to be thought of as . . . | Brilliance Brilliant | Wisdom Wise | Courage Courageous | Faithfulness Faithful | Loyalty Loyal |
| Most Enjoyed Phase of a project . . . | Designing theoretical solutions | Designing theoretical solutions, developing first prototype | Developing and expanding the model | Refining the basic system and maximizing it | Maintaining the basic model and keeping it under control |
| Oriented in a New Situation by . . . | Theory | Process | Goal | Results | Control |
| Creativity . . . | Original . . . Want to start with a blank sheet of paper | Original . . . Want to start with a blank sheet of paper | Adaptive . . . Want to start with existing models and improve | Adaptive . . . Want to start with existing models and improve | Adaptive . . . Want to start with existing models and improve |
| Burnout Point . . . | When a problem is solved theoretically | 7/8 of the way through the development of the prototype | When the goal is reached or after 2 years on a single project | 4–5 years into a project . . . when things are going too smoothly | 20+ years or when there is disloyalty on the part of the team leader or peers |

Everyone has a burnout point. As you can see from the Role Preference Inventory, you can begin to predict where your burnout point is even if you aren't dealing with the death of a dream at the same time. Many people reach a burnout point in their work, but are not aware of what to do about it, how it happened, or how to deal with it. If this is where you find yourself, it is very important for you to identify what phases your various home and workplace projects are currently in, and what your preferred phase is.

If your preferred phase is the design and development phase, and the prototype was done years ago, the model has been put together, and it's into a maintenance phase, no wonder you're burned out. You need to get out of that project some way and get back into a design/development phase where your natural energy can be restored. *Anyone operating out of their natural phase will experience burnout.* The further you're operating out of your phase, the greater energy it takes to discipline yourself to go to work every day, or work on the project, and the smaller amount of personal fulfillment you receive from it.

That deadly combination of high energy spent and little emotional reward leads very quickly to the feeling of burnout. Burnout simply feels like *Is it worth it? Why would I keep doing this? I don't think I've got what it takes to keep going. I'd rather stay here in bed in the morning. I just look forward to going to bed at night. I can't keep this up for very long.*

Because of your natural discipline which you learned in childhood and early adulthood, you may go for months or even years in a state of burnout, but sooner or later you are in an extreme state of exhaustion. You may still be on the job, but the light has gone out of your eyes and your heart begins asking, *Can I see myself growing old doing this every day?* And the answer comes back like flashing neon signs, "No! No! No!"

But then the questions begin: *Where would I go if I wasn't here? What are my options? How would I pay the bills? What would my parents/my spouse/other people think of me if I stopped doing what I'm doing?* Again, the questions can blur the path required to get out of the phase that is causing such burnout.

Caught in this state of fatigue and burnout you may try to put on a mask. "I'm OK, everything's OK." And you try to keep going to work, do your job, stay involved, make money, pay the bills, even though inside there is an enormous amount of frustration, pain, and confusion. It takes tremendous energy to keep going in the wrong phase, and even more when you attempt to keep up an emotional mask, making the rest of the world think you're OK when, in fact, you're dying inside.

Bottom line: in a state of burnout you may feel like a "walking zombie," as though you've been without sleep for sixty hours. It's difficult to keep putting one foot in front of the other. At the same time, the world around you may believe that you have the "ideal job, the ideal family, the ideal life." No one seems to care that you are being ground up in the middle of all this. As a result, the questions start blurring the vision. Questions such as, *Am I just being used? Will I ever make it? Have I got the energy to keep going? Is that pain in my chest a heart attack? Am I going to grow old feeling this way?*

These and other questions of midlife begin to speak very loudly, begin to demand attention. And all of a sudden there is a panic in the answer that comes back, triggering the midlife reevaluation: *I've got to make some changes. I don't know what they are, I don't know how I'm going to do it. I don't know who to talk to, who to trust, but I've got to make some changes or I'm going to die here in this storm. I don't know where to go, or what to do. I don't like letting people know I'm this confused, this lonely. I feel like no one understands where I am. I feel like there's just no place to go for help. I'm exhausted.*

---

## Heart Probe:

Does this sound like you? Perhaps you are at the point where you've got a disillusioned dream and a burned-out emotional system and energy level and are saying to yourself, *I've got to make some changes or I'm going to die in this fatigued, dreamless state of exhaustion.* If so, keep breathing, because there is hope in the Midlife Reevaluation Process (Map Point 8).

---

Note: Let me stop here just a second to tell you that, so far, I've been trying to let you know that I understand some of where your mind and heart are at the moment if, in fact, your dream has been disillusioned and you're experiencing a state of deep fatigue. I've also tried to help those who are trying to help you understand the blur, the lack of clarity that you are experiencing, so that they can empathize with you more accurately.

The book does become more hopeful, but I wanted to create the picture so you would see that I understand where you are. It does get better. There is hope!

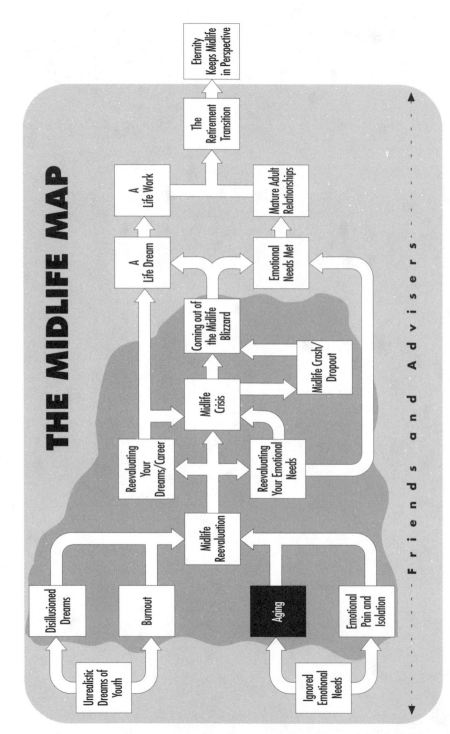

THE MIDLIFE MAP

Unrealistic Dreams of Youth → Disillusioned Dreams

Burnout

Midlife Reevaluation

Reevaluating Your Dreams/Career

Midlife Crisis

Coming out of the Midlife Blizzard

A Life Dream

A Life Work

The Retirement Transition

Eternity Keeps Midlife in Perspective

Aging

Ignored Emotional Needs → Emotional Pain and Isolation

Reevaluating Your Emotional Needs

Midlife Crash/Dropout

Emotional Needs Met

Mature Adult Relationships

◄- - - - - - Friends and Advisers - - - - - - ►

© Bobb Biehl 1993

# Map Point 6: Aging: The Third Midlife Reevaluation "Trigger"

*The aging process catches up with everyone.*

Minnie Remembers by Donna Swanson

God, my hands are old.
I've never said that out loud before
but they are.  I was so proud of them once.
They were soft
like the velvet smoothness of a
firm, ripe peach.
Now the softness is more like
worn out sheets
or withered leaves.
When did these slender, graceful hands
become gnarled, shrunken claws?
When, God?
They lie here in my lap;
naked reminders of this worn out
body that has served me too well.

How long has it been since someone
touched me?
Twenty years?
Twenty years I've been a widow.
Respected.

Smiled at.
But never touched.
Never held so close that loneliness
was blotted out.

I remember how my mother used to hold
me, God.
When I was hurt in spirit or flesh,
she would gather me close,
stroke my silky hair,
and caress my back with her warm
hands.  Oh God, I'm so lonely!

I remember the first boy who ever
kissed me.
We were both so new at that!
The taste of young lips and popcorn,
the feeling inside of mysteries to come.
I remember Hank and the babies.
How else can I remember them
but together?
For out of the fumbling, awkward attempts
of new lovers came the babies.
And, as they grew, so did our love.
And, God, Hank didn't seem to mind
if my body thickened and faded a little.
He still loved it
and touched it.
And we didn't mind if we were no longer beautiful.
And it felt so good.
And the children hugged me a lot.
Oh God, I'm lonely!

God, why didn't we raise the kids
to be silly and affectionate
as well as dignified and proper?
You see, they do their duty.
They drive up in their fine cars.
They come to my room
to pay their respects.
They chatter brightly and reminisce.

But they don't touch me.
They call me Mom, or Mother or Grandma.
Never Minnie.
My mother called me Minnie.
So did my friends.
Hank called me Minnie, too.
But they're gone.
And so is Minnie.
Only Grandma is here.
And God, she is lonely!

© 1978 from *Mind Song* published by Upper Room, 1908 Grand Avenue, Nashville, Tennessee 37202. May be reprinted by permission only, by contacting Donna Swanson, R.1, Williamsport, IN 47995. Phone (317) 764-4225

If you want to get a realistic view of how powerful a human being is, go off by yourself sometime and try to force time to stop. Time stops for no one—queen or president. Nor does it stop for the pro athlete, the beauty queen, the singer at the top of the charts, the actor who just got an Emmy or an Oscar. Time stops for no one. I remember my dad saying, "The longer I live the faster time seems to fly, year after year. Each year goes faster than the last one." Here enters the third trigger of the midlife reevaluation process.

## Am I "Over the Hill"?

The hair begins to gray. The crow's feet begin to show up. Weight is five times more difficult to control. It is harder to stay in shape, even with a new, slightly broader shape you are trying to stay in today. Your energy level, your stamina, is just not the same.

You wake up one morning and ask yourself, as you look in the mirror, *Am I growing old?* People reassure you, "Oh, you're not getting old!" But slowly, day by day, you begin coming to grips with midlife. You're no longer the whiz kid with lofty potential. Now you're an adult facing raw reality—a mortgage and kids you can't figure out how to put through college.

Some have early health problems, while others profess that they're aging gracefully—but relentlessly. Some say, "I'm fighting the aging process every single step of the way," and start frequenting beauty counters in every department store.

63

Aging in a youth culture is especially challenging, where everyone is supposed to look young, healthy, happy, carefree. And when the disillusioned dreams, burnout, and the aging process start, it's very hard to appear young and energetic. Even if you are in a state of total denial, you will ultimately come to a very abrupt realization that "the old gray mare ain't what she used to be." You may not admit ever thinking a single thought about getting old, but then the reality of those aging around you, or the death of someone very important to you forces you to come to grips with the fact that you cannot stop the hands of time.

WARNING: In this period of life many people encounter a major chemical imbalance. You may be experiencing a loss of energy, not because of the natural aging process everyone experiences, but because of such a chemical imbalance. If you suffer from recurring headaches or other painful symptoms, consult your medical doctor.

You may be tempted to think that you can retard the aging process. You'll try harder, exercise more, eat less, be more disciplined. But as the midlife reevaluation starts, the reality of aging can no longer be denied. You begin to lose hope that some of your physical dreams will ever be realized, because you are getting older and older. The reality begins to set in that you are in a midlife phase, whether you want to be or not.

The aging process sparks its own set of questions, such as: *What will my personality be like as an old person? Will I die in a continuing care retirement home? Will my kids care if I have to live with them? What will I look like when I'm old? Will I lose all my hair? Will I be able to pay my way? Will people still like me?*

If you feel people like you because of how you look or what you are able to do for them, facing the aging process is especially difficult. You begin to ask yourself, *Why do people like me? Why do they want me around? Because I win the games? If I didn't win the games, would they still want me around? Because of my beautiful body? If I develop cellulite or get hurt and can't perform, will anyone want me around at all?* This is the terror of the aging process, particularly if your sense of self-worth has been based on your public self.

For you, it is a time to reevaluate. The aging process may feel like "I think I can, I think I can . . . I thought I could, I thought I could . . . I never will, I never will." How will you begin to develop your interior core, your character, your personality, your ability to relate to people, and not feel as if your life is over?

**Heart Probe:**

How fearful are you about the thought of growing old?

How dependent are you on how you look in order to feel accepted by others?

If your mask has been a critical part of your self-worth—your image, your youthful face and body—it's very important that you begin laying out a step-by-step process for developing your inner personality. Develop your ability to relate to people based on who you are, and not what you do or how you look.

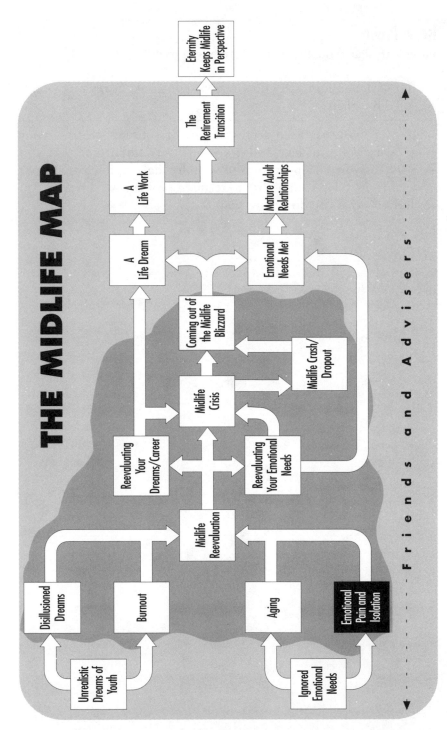

THE MIDLIFE MAP

Unrealistic Dreams of Youth

Disillusioned Dreams

Burnout

Reevaluating Your Dreams/Career

Midlife Reevaluation

Midlife Crisis

Coming out of the Midlife Blizzard

A Life Dream

A Life Work

The Retirement Transition

Eternity Keeps Midlife in Perspective

Reevaluating Your Emotional Needs

Midlife Crash/Dropout

Emotional Needs Met

Mature Adult Relationships

Aging

Emotional Pain and Isolation

Ignored Emotional Needs

- - - - - - Friends and Advisers - - - - - -

© Bobb Biehl 1993

# Map Point 7: Emotional Pain and Isolation: The Fourth Midlife Reevaluation "Trigger"

Our unconscious assumption is that if we could just reach certain life goals, our emotional needs would be met. When we become aware that the meeting of our goals has not met these needs, we begin to wonder, *Will my emotional needs ever really be met?*

Emotional pain is in many cases far more painful than physical pain. If you don't agree, ask a mother or father watching a son or daughter suffer. But until you find yourself in an emotional blizzard, you may have assumed that physical pain is the only debilitating pain and that the pain caused by unmet emotional needs really doesn't hurt that much. Sure, you have needs for love or acceptance or respect, but the real pain is physical pain. It is a jolting reality when you discover that your unmet emotional needs are causing great headache-producing, groaning, sad, lonely pain.

Recently a major research firm was commissioned to do a three quarters of a million dollars research study. They were asked to find the greatest needs of the human heart. Their research showed that the number-one need in the minds and hearts of people was loneliness. In those lonely hearts lies the feeling that no one else really understands who they are or what they're experiencing.

But the second greatest pain uncovered by the researchers was described as "something is missing." The person could not describe what the missing component was. They simply knew there was something in their lives that was missing. They felt hollow and needy, but didn't understand what would fill the void.

As mentioned in chapter 4, there are only eight emotional needs that people have:

1. The need to be loved.
2. The need to make a significant difference.
3. The need to be admired.
4. The need to be recognized for who you are as a person.
5. The need to be appreciated.
6. The need to be secure.
7. The need to be respected.
8. The need to be accepted.

It's in the early midlife years that you begin to realize that money, power, position, sex—whatever it is you may have pursued to meet your emotional needs—is not meeting those needs, and you begin to experience enormous emotional pain or void or hurt. When you realize that these needs are unmet and will not be met in the ways you have conventionally gone about it, this question begins to haunt your very heart: *Can I face growing old without these emotional needs met?*

All too often, this begins a rather frantic search for ways to get your needs met. You turn first to your spouse, and then your friends, your mentors, your therapist. And when those needs are still not met, there is the temptation to turn to someone of the opposite sex in an illicit affair—anything to have your emotional needs met, because the lack of respect, or the lack of love, or the lack of significance is too painful to abide.

Be aware of the fact that this is a point at which you are the most vulnerable to an affair. This is when the person who seems to meet the needs that your life mate cannot meet becomes very attractive. And you need to set up a few warning fences that say "be cautious" at this point.

## Many Reasons Needs Go Unmet

Your legitimate emotional needs may go unmet for any number of reasons but following are a few common examples:

The person who has typically, historically been the person to meet your needs gets sick, dies, moves away, or in some other way stops meeting those needs.

There are major differences between you and your spouse in terms of pace, values, social level, ability. One man I know is an extraordinarily fast-paced individual and his wife is not, and it sets them both up for unmet needs.

You may be living with an egocentric person, a person who assumes life revolves around him/her. There are at least three possible combinations here:

(1) Two egocentric people, who may also be relatively inflexible, find it extremely difficult to get needs met by each other for rather obvious reasons.

(2) You have two people both expecting the other to meet their needs, but have little capacity to give in return.

(3) A wife spends time meeting the husband's needs, and the husband spends time meeting the husband's needs, and it puts the wife in a vulnerable position.

You live by a demanding schedule, which makes awareness and consistent meeting of a spouse's needs very difficult at times.

Many couples marry to have their emotional needs met. However, this is just not realistic. Your spouse may never have been able to meet your needs adequately. It is also true that many times your needs change over the course of a decade or two, and the person who has been meeting your needs in one decade may find it very difficult to even know what your needs are when you get into your late thirties and early forties.

It is also unhealthy to expect that your mate will meet *all* your needs. Some of your needs are met by friends, some by parents, some by colleagues, some by buddies, some by mentors, but not all of your needs should, or can, be met by one person. To the extent that you expect one person to meet all your needs, you set yourself up for disappointment later.

Another reality is that opposites attract early in the marriage but find it difficult to communicate later. The more you and your mate are alike, the easier it is to communicate.

One of the main reasons people have unmet emotional needs is that they are simply unaware of how they feel about anything. Perhaps you were raised in a stoic family and you actually don't know how you feel. If this is you, take the following assignment very seriously, and begin to define how you feel at any given moment so that you can communicate this clearly to those trying to help you understand and deal with your midlife blizzard.

# I Feel Checklist

How to use this checklist:
1. Read through the following list and circle each word which expresses an emotion you are currently feeling.
2. Read through the list again and double circle those you feel more intensely than the others.
3. Of those words you have circled twice, put a star by the ten you feel most intensely.
4. Of the ten words you starred, double star the top three emotions you are experiencing.
5. Finally, triple star the single word that expresses the most dominant emotion you are currently experiencing.

| | | |
|---|---|---|
| Abandoned | At ease | Claustrophobic |
| Abused | Attractive | Comfortable |
| Admired | Awed | Committed |
| Adored | Awkward | Competitive |
| Affectionate | Bad | Concerned |
| Affirmed | Baffled | Confident |
| Afraid | Bashful | Confused |
| Aggressive | Battered/Bruised | Consoled |
| Alarmed | Behind | Content |
| Alert | Belittled | Courageous |
| Alienated | Benevolent | Creative |
| Alive | Betrayed | Cynical |
| Alone | Bewildered | Daring |
| Amazed | Bitter | Defeated |
| Ambivalent | Bored | Defensive |
| Amused | Bound | Degraded |
| Angry | Brave | Dejected |
| Annoyed | Brilliant | Delighted |
| Antagonistic | Broke | Dependent |
| Anticipating | Buried | Depressed |
| Anxious | Burned-out | Despair |
| Apathetic | Callous | Despised |
| Appealing | Capable | Destined |
| Appreciated | Cared For | Determined |
| Apprehensive | Challenged | Devastated |
| Approved | Cheated | Disappointed |

| | | |
|---|---|---|
| Disciplined | Foggy | Important |
| Discontent | Foolish | Inadequate |
| Disgusted | Forgiving | Incapable |
| Dishonest | Forlorn | Included |
| Disillusioned | Fragmented | Indecisive |
| Disloyal | Free | Independent |
| Dismal | Friendly | Indifferent |
| Dismayed | Frightened | Indignant |
| Disorganized | Frustrated | Ineffective |
| Disoriented | Fulfilled | Inexperienced |
| Dissatisfied | Fun Focused | Infatuated |
| Down and Out | Furious | Inferior |
| Drifting | Futile | Influential |
| Driven | Generous | Infuriated |
| Drowning | Glad | Inhibited |
| Dry | Gloomy | Insecure |
| Dumb | Good | Insignificant |
| Eager | Graceful | Inspired |
| Edgy | Gratified | Intelligent |
| Effective | Great | Interested |
| Efficient | Guilty | Intimidated |
| Elated | Hand-cuffed | Irritated |
| Embarrassed | Happy | Isolated |
| Empty | Hated | Jealous |
| Enchanted | Hectic | Jolly |
| Enthusiastic | Held Back | Joyful |
| Envious | Helpless | Left Behind |
| Esteemed | Hollow | Lethargic |
| Estrangement | Honest | Like a Nobody |
| Excited | Honored | Liked |
| Exhausted | Hopeful | Listless |
| Failure | Hopeless | Loathed |
| Faithful | Horrified | Lonely |
| Fat | Hostile | Lost |
| Fatherless | Humiliated | Loved |
| Fatigued | Hyper | Loyal |
| Fearful | Idolized | Lustful |
| Fed up | Ignored | Mad |
| Focused | Impatient | Mismatched |

| | | |
|---|---|---|
| Misplaced | Ready | Superior |
| Misunderstood | Regret | Sure |
| Mixed-up | Rejected | Suspicious |
| Moody | Relaxed | Sympathetic |
| Naive | Relieved | Teachable |
| Negative | Reluctant | Tempted |
| Neglected | Resentment | Tender |
| Nervous | Resigned | Tense |
| Numb | Resistant | Tentative |
| Obnoxious | Respected | Terrified |
| Old | Responsible | Threatened |
| On Track | Restless | Timid |
| Optimistic | Revengeful | Tired |
| Optionless | Sad | Torn-Up |
| Out of Control | Satisfied | Trapped |
| Out of Shape | Scared | Treadmilled |
| Overcommitted | Scattered | Turned On |
| Overweight | Secure | Unappreciated |
| Overwhelmed | Self-Conscious | Unattractive |
| Pained | Sensitive | Uncertain |
| Panicky | Sexy | Uncomfortable |
| Passed By | Shame | Undereducated |
| Passionate | Shocked | Underpaid |
| Patient | Shuffled | Underrated |
| Peaceful | Shy | Understaffed |
| Perplexed | Sick | Undisciplined |
| Pitied | Significant | Undiscovered |
| Pleased | Smart | Unfaithful |
| Popular | Smothered | Unhappy |
| Positive | Stable | Unheard |
| Pressured | Stagnant | Unlimited |
| Professional | Stifled | Unloved |
| Progress | Streetwise | Unneeded |
| Prosperous | Stretched | Unpopular |
| Protected | Strong | Unprofessional |
| Proud | Stunned | Unsexy |
| Provoked | Stunted | Unsure |
| Puzzled | Successful | Unwanted |
| Ragged | Sullen | Unwise |

| | | |
|---|---|---|
| Upset | Warm | Worn Out |
| Used | Washed Up | Worried |
| Useless | Weak | Worthless |
| Valiant | Weary | Worthy |
| Venturesome | Weepy | Wrongly Accused |
| Vibrant | Wise | Yearning |
| Wanted | Withdrawn | Zealous |

## Heart Probe:

In your heart of hearts, where no one else sees, what are your unmet needs? ( Make a list.)

From your perspective, why are these needs going unmet?

Write out your emotional needs so you can get a more objective look at your needs and why they're not being met. This will clarify what is in your heart far more than you can by simply thinking about it and letting the questions drift around in your mind and heart.

My greatest emotional need is for _____

The person(s) I wish would meet these needs:

NOTE: Read *Why You Do What You Do* for further study on the subject of emotional needs.

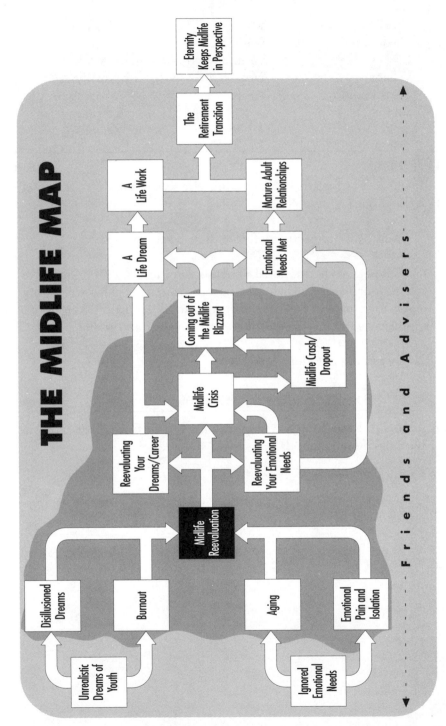

# THE MIDLIFE MAP

Unrealistic Dreams of Youth → Disillusioned Dreams

Burnout

Disillusioned Dreams → Midlife Reevaluation ← Burnout

Aging → Midlife Reevaluation

Ignored Emotional Needs → Emotional Pain and Isolation → Midlife Reevaluation

Midlife Reevaluation → Reevaluating Your Dreams/Career

Midlife Reevaluation → Reevaluating Your Emotional Needs

Reevaluating Your Dreams/Career → Midlife Crisis

Reevaluating Your Emotional Needs → Midlife Crisis

Midlife Crisis → Coming out of the Midlife Blizzard

Midlife Crisis → Midlife Crash/Dropout

Coming out of the Midlife Blizzard → A Life Dream

Midlife Crash/Dropout → Emotional Needs Met

A Life Dream → A Life Work

Emotional Needs Met → Mature Adult Relationships

A Life Work → The Retirement Transition

Mature Adult Relationships → The Retirement Transition

The Retirement Transition → Eternity Keeps Midlife in Perspective

- - - - - Friends and Advisers - - - - -

© Bobb Biehl 1993

# Map Point 8: Midlife Reevaluation

Reevaluation is a very healthy, helpful process. Refocusing our dreams and relating to others in a way that gets our needs met helps us avoid a midlife crisis or midlife crash/dropout. Midlife Reevaluation can realistically be seen as a "warning track" to midlife crisis and midlife dropout!

The "warning track" in a baseball park is the dirt space beyond the outfield but before the wall. When an outfielder is running back toward the fence to catch a deep fly ball and feels the warning track beneath his spikes he knows that he is about to hit the wall and needs to be far more cautious in his backward speed.

Midlife reevaluation is a healthy—and I emphasize "healthy"—correction process that we go through to avoid midlife crisis and, eventually, even potentially, midlife dropout! This reevaluation has been triggered by disappointed dreams, burnout, the aging process, and unmet emotional needs, leaving you with a feeling of having limited energy, uncertain direction, feeling older and older, and a sense of being alone with no one who really understands or cares what is happening. As mentioned earlier, this is frequently because we have not developed the ability to open our hearts to people in an intimate way and tell them we are struggling to survive. We wear a mask which says, "Everything's OK. I'm fine."

However, between thirty-five and forty-five—sometimes earlier, sometimes a bit later—it begins to be obvious that something has to change. You have to make a change—a fairly substantial change—in your lifestyle, your dreams, your exercise program, your relational style. In some ways, you have to change because you simply cannot face growing old the way you are. This is when you begin to take the midlife reevaluation process very, very seriously.

Some dreams need to be reevaluated and then discarded at this phase of life. Some lifelong dreams just simply are not going to happen.

"When the folks who have dreamed for years about a big summer house where all the kids would flock finally accept that they don't have the money and the kids have other plans, they release a lot of tension. This kind of surrender is very productive, because dreams that run counter to reality waste a lot of energy" (From "Midlife Myths" by Winifred Gallagher, *The Atlantic Monthly*, May 1993, 53).

It is important to come to grips with the fact that life does change, that not all dreams are ours to grasp. But we can still press forward. We need a *progressively* accurate view of ourselves and our resources and a commitment to achieve some new significant dreams. We are capable, over the next thirty or forty years, of giving, expending, contributing, touching, shaping many things.

Let me pause here a second to reassure you that all midlife re-evaluation does not end in midlife crisis or dropout. One of the reasons for this book is to help you avoid Map Points 11, 12, and 13 altogether. But if you simply ignore the feelings you have by the time you get to Map Point 8 in the midlife map, you're going to find that you do drift your way toward crisis and dropout.

The value in the midlife reevaluation is not simply to avoid midlife crisis and dropout, but rather to optimize and strengthen the significance of your life contribution and your day-to-day relationships. This process is marked by questions like: *What changes can I make in my life that will really make a difference? What could I do differently? Should I quit the company and go back and teach school? What changes will get my needs met and turn my dreams into reality?* These are healthy changes which take into account the impact on your family, your spouse, and your reputation.

## Midlife Blizzard: The Further You Go, the Denser It Gets

If you sense you're in midlife reevaluation, chances are you feel like you're flying through the clouds on instruments alone, and you are even beginning to question your instruments at certain points. No matter how powerful, no matter how strong, no matter how capable you are, you start slowing life down because you don't know where you're going, and you don't want to run smack-dab, full speed, into a mountain.

It's really important to see that the midlife blizzard does not last forever. It starts with Map Points 4, 5, 6, and 7, and ends with Map Point 13, and there will come a day when you will come out of this blizzard, but right now there is very limited visibility, very little sense of future, very little sense of bearings. The blizzard is so great that time and eternity seem to be irrelevant; friends, spouse, therapists, and mentors seem not to understand, and you feel all alone, trapped in the blizzard. This is not true, but it feels that way, nonetheless. Remember: there is hope!

Midlife emotional pain turns any person into a self-centered individual, in a similar way that physical pain does. If you are used to high energy, clear goals, a bright future, an energetic body, and friends who care, finding yourself in the middle of a midlife reevaluation with low energy, blurry future, no clear sense of direction, a feeling of aging by the day, and feeling as though no one really understands or cares, brings on a loneliness of soul that is very, very difficult for others to comprehend.

This may be the first time since childhood that you have experienced such a sense of loneliness, a sense that no one really understands where you are, who you are, what you're experiencing, what you're going through. And no matter how hard you try to talk, no matter how definitive you try to be, there are simply no answers at this given point in time.

I remember the first day I felt this loneliness, personally. Up to that point, I had probably felt lonely two days in my entire lifetime. But all of a sudden I had this overwhelming sense of loneliness and sadness, and I couldn't identify what was happening. Eventually, I realized that there are many kinds of loneliness.

1. Social loneliness: typically thought of as being alone, separated from your friends.
2. Financial loneliness: when you are in a financial situation you can't tell anyone else about, or no one seems to bear the burden but you.
3. Family and marriage loneliness: when you are away from spouse or family.

4. Physical loneliness: when you long for someone to hold and touch you, and care for you physically.
5. Professional loneliness: when you have lots of friends socially, lots of time with your family, but no one knows where you are professionally.
6. Spiritual loneliness: when you are in a certain point in your spiritual journey, and you know of no one else who is at that same crossroads.

*Loneliness of Soul*

There is a loneliness
which can only be called a loneliness of heart,
or a loneliness of soul.
It is a loneliness you feel
even though you have many friends
that you say hello to day to day,
your family—you kiss them good-bye every morning.
There is a sense, a feeling of drowning
in the midlife issues that you're experiencing.

There is no one
to hear your heart as it calls out,
as you scream silently for someone to help you
redefine your dreams
or meet your unmet emotional dreams.

It's a loneliness with which very few can empathize
unless they have walked a similar path.

It's in the middle of this pain and loneliness that many people experience depression, sometimes for the first time. In the book *Why You Do What You Do* depression is described as "drowning in our negative childhood fears." Often, when you're in this stage of midlife blizzard, childhood fears come back to haunt you. *Will I ever do it right? Am I adequate? Will I ever be safe? Will anyone ever really like me? Am I going to be intimidated and dominated? Will I ever really make a significant difference?* And whenever these childhood fears come back, depression accompanies them.

Let's stop here a second. This sounds kind of bleak, doesn't it?

Well, it *is* bleak. But I'm here to give you hope that in the middle of all this, as you redefine your dreams and as you find ways to relate to people in meaningful ways, and get your emotional needs met, you will come back out of this blizzard and there will come a day when you will see clearly once again. Remember: there is hope!

However, in the middle of the pain you become very self-centered, and it is very important for you to be aware of just how self-centered you may become. You are in so much pain you want to talk about it all the time. You want to dominate conversations with talk about yourself. Those trying to relate to you can understand physical pain. If you cut off your finger, they would understand why you would want to talk about it, why you would want to discuss it, why you would want to process it. But, unable to see what's in your heart, they find it difficult to understand why you seem to feel this great need to talk about your emotional needs and dreams without ever seeming to come to resolution. Just when they seem to answer one of your questions, you've got 1/3 more waiting in line to be addressed!

It's about now in the process that you may begin to question your long-term values. You begin abandoning some lifelong yardsticks, reevaluating all values, shifting your paradigms, questioning truth, and questioning even the absolutes that though spoken 2,000 years ago in scriptural times, have been true for all time. These values begin to blur and mix and spin, and it's very difficult to keep them in perspective because of the pain that you experience at the moment. Just as it would be very difficult to discuss theological issues if you had cut off your hand and had not had medical treatment, it is very difficult to discuss the theological implications of midlife with your pastor or mate or friend, because the pain is so intense.

Your entire being seems to be screaming out, *I can't dance any faster!* Your whole system begs and pleads for an answer to the question, *Is it worth it?* You join the writer of Ecclesiastes in saying, "Vanity, vanity, all is vanity." These have been midlife feelings since ancient days.

Your confidence begins to wobble because of a sense of lost predictability. You try to grasp for your dreams, and yet they seem like illusions. You try to get your emotional needs met, and the very persons that you hoped would meet the needs can't even understand where you are. The pain grows intense, and your interest in reducing that emotional pain grows, and you become very self-centered, finding it very difficult to give, nurture, help, or encourage anyone around you. It's in this confusion, in this frustration, in this pain, in this anguish, that midlife reevaluation takes place.

## Objective Assessment

It's critical that you redefine and adjust your thinking one question at a time. You ask yourself questions such as, *Why, how, and when do I settle for a lesser dream than I had imagined? Would it be premature, wise, or just realistic to pursue a new dream?* There's a constant struggle for the balance between protecting your dreams and letting them go, between redefining and settling.

Please consider seriously taking a day, a week, a month away for an intense reevaluation. Get back to your roots, perhaps back to the place where you feel the safest, emotionally. Back to your hometown, to your favorite cabin or lake, out in the woods, by the ocean. Get away by yourself for a couple of days and really begin to focus your mind and heart on Map Points 9 and 10.

---

### Heart Probe:

Would you candidly admit to yourself that you are squarely in the middle of midlife reevaluation?

---

As panicky as it feels, millions have been there before and have worked their way to a positive, healthy solution in the end. It does not last forever, it will clear up. The sky will be blue again. The storm will stop. The blizzard will cease. There is hope!

The next two Map Points, the next two knots on the rope, will do two things:

> (1) begin redefining your life dream and your career, and
> (2) begin to identify what you really need emotionally from those who love you and care the most about you.

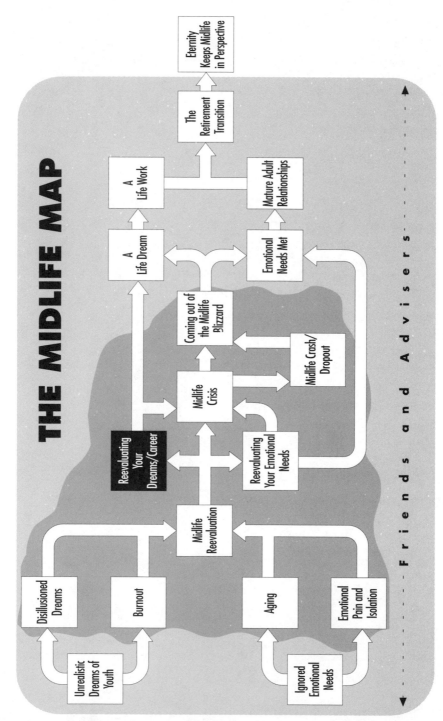

# THE MIDLIFE MAP

Eternity Keeps Midlife in Perspective

The Retirement Transition

A Life Work

A Life Dream

Mature Adult Relationships

Coming out of the Midlife Blizzard

Emotional Needs Met

Midlife Crisis

Midlife Crash/ Dropout

Reevaluating Your Dreams/Career

Reevaluating Your Emotional Needs

Midlife Reevaluation

Disillusioned Dreams

Burnout

Aging

Emotional Pain and Isolation

Unrealistic Dreams of Youth

Ignored Emotional Needs

- - - - - Friends and Advisers - - - - -

© Bobb Biehl 1993

# Map Point 9: Reevaluating Your Dreams/Career

Here is where we begin to reassess the possibility of dreaming a new dream, of starting a new position, or even starting an entirely new career.

To get started in the dream and career defining/redefining process, please work your way through six very specific steps with me. You may find all six steps helpful, or perhaps one or two will seem particularly significant. Take what you need to help you redefine your dreams and career today.

STEP 1.     Complete the dream questions.
STEP 2.     Fill out the Life Focus Chart.
STEP 3.     Rate your dream, your field, your organization, your position.
STEP 4.     Answer the Career Change Questions.
STEP 5.     Define success for yourself (see if you agree with my definition).
STEP 6.     Read the Time Pressure material and give yourself the freedom to gain a big picture of the time required for this kind of definition.

# Dream Questions

*1. God:*

What three changes in me would most please our Eternal God in His holy heaven?

    1.

    2.

    3.

*2. Dream/Purpose:*

What can I do to make the most significant difference for God in my lifetime?

Why am I on the earth?

What is the very best organizational context for my dream?

*3. Primary Result:*

What is the single best measurable indicator that I am making progress toward my dream?

*4. Life Priorities:*

If I could accomplish only three measurable priorities before I die, what would they be?

    1.

    2.

    3.

*5. Ten-year Focus:*

If I could accomplish only three measurable priorities in the next ten years that would make a 50 percent difference in my lifelong contribution, what would they be?

    1.

    2.

    3.

*6. Annual Focus:*

SINGLE WORD FOCUS: What single word best captures the focus of my next year?


OPPORTUNITY: Where was my greatest success last year? Why?


What three steps could I take now to take full advantage of my "Window of Opportunity" this coming year?


LAND MINES: What three "land mines" or "roadblocks" need my immediate attention?

What have I been "worrying/praying" most about in the past thirty days?

What three changes could reduce my "risk" by 50 percent?

    1.

    2.

    3.

3/YEAR/50 percent: If I could only accomplish three measurable priorities in the next twelve months that would make a 50 percent difference in my contribution in the next ten years, which three things would I most want to accomplish?

    1.

    2.

    3.

*7. Quarterly Focus:*

What three priorities could I accomplish in the next ninety days to make a 50 percent difference in the results I see by the end of the year?

    1.

    2.

3.

### 8. Organization:

What three changes could I make to see a 50 percent difference in our morale as a family or team?

1.

2.

3.

### 9. Cash:

If I had to cut my budget 21 percent, what would be the first three things to go?

1.

2.

3.

If I got a surprise gift of 21 percent of my budget, what three things would I do immediately?

1.

2.

3.

### 10. Quality:

What three changes could improve the quality of my work by 50 percent in the next twelve months?

1.

2.

3.

## Life Focus

Does it ever seem to you that your life is composed of constant "roller coaster" ups and downs, or major zigzags as you move, first one direction, then another? Without a clear decision about whether you are going to New York or Los Angeles, every intersection is a separate stressful decision. Once you say, "I'm on my way to L.A.," a thousand intersection decisions have already been made. And once you have your life in focus, many day-to-day "intersection" decisions are obvious. Without life focus each is a more or less stressful decision.

We humans typically avoid, at nearly all costs, the thought of our own death. At the same time, we each have "secret" but often foggy or unwritten plans about what we want to do before we die!

The Life Focus Chart is a profoundly simple, fun, relatively easy way of helping you gain a crystal-clear, lifelong perspective. Once you have completed the Life Focus Chart, you can regain your perspective in about ten minutes—anywhere, anytime, for the rest of your life!

|    | Be! | Do! | Have! | Help! |
|----|-----|-----|-------|-------|
| 1  |     |     |       |       |
| 2  |     |     |       |       |
| 3  |     |     |       |       |
| 4  |     |     |       |       |
| 5  |     |     |       |       |
| 6  |     |     |       |       |
| 7  |     |     |       |       |
| 8  |     |     |       |       |
| 9  |     |     |       |       |
| 10 |     |     |       |       |

Don't panic if you can't fill all ten slots in some column. Ten is the maximum, not the minimum! Even if you can only fill in one box, you are making progress. You may prefer to take several hours, spread over a month or two and involve conversations with a spouse, close friend, or mentor to complete your Life Focus Chart.

Let's begin! (You may want to copy this chart on a flip-chart sized piece of paper, or enter it into your computer.)

Instructions for Life Focus Chart:

*Column One: BE!*
Finish the phrase, "Before I die I want to BE _____."

(Examples: honest, loyal husband/wife, committed Christian, millionaire, board member, etc.) What are your highest personal values, your most desired character traits, your most coveted roles? What do you desire to be the "essence" of who you are as a person? Fill in the "BE" column with a maximum of ten of your highest ideals.

*Column Two: DO!*

Finish the phrase, "Before I die, I want to DO these things _____."

(Example: Climb Mt. Everest, build a home, start a company, own a certain antique, write a book, travel around the world, hold my grandchildren, teach or learn painting, etc.) Your "DO" entries don't have to be worthy of a Nobel Prize nomination, but if they are what you actually want to do before you die, write them down!

If you have a difficult time getting started in this section, you may want to ask yourself, "If I could do any ten things I wanted to do before I die, if I had unlimited time, energy, money, education, staff, if I knew I couldn't fail—and God told me to do as I choose—what ten things would I want to do?" Fill in a maximum of ten measurable life "DO" items.

*Column Three: HAVE!*

What ten things would you like to "HAVE" before you die? (Examples: A house, new car, degree, getaway cabin, secretary, your own company, etc.) You can also write down things you already have. For example, I put down that I want to have the home I currently own. I would be happy in this house for the rest of my life. It's OK to be happy with any possession you have and want to keep having. Fill in the "HAVE" column as much as possible.

*Column Four: HELP!*

What ten individuals, organizations, and causes do you most want to help in a significant way before you die? (Examples: Your children, parents, nieces, nephews, brother, sister, Boy Scouts, your church, world hunger organizations, etc.) Who do you really want to see "win" in life? Which individuals, projects, or causes do you want to see gain strength because you have lived? Fill in the "HELP" column.

Additional thoughts:

When you get your dreams written down on this sheet, you may choose to keep this information confidential, or you may decide to share it with a close friend.

You may also want to go back to each column and put a star by the single most important item in each column. If you could only accomplish one of the ten, which one would you accomplish?

You can also use this same process for a group to ask questions such as "What ten things do we want to accomplish during the life of our group?"

On each future birthday, or on New Year's Day, or when you are feeling generally "out of focus," pull this sheet out of your "Focus file" and in about ten minutes regain your life perspective! You can do this anywhere, anytime, for the rest of your life.

These are some of your dreams. They represent the difference you want to make in life. This is what you want to BE, DO, HAVE, and who you want to HELP! Let's call all of these your dreams.

## Rating Your Dream, Your Field, Your Organization, Your Position

Ideally your professional dream should fit your field, organization, and position as precisely as a perfectly round peg in a perfectly round hole of the exact same size.

Complete the following:

I would describe my professional dream as:

_____

_____

I would describe the field I am in (the expertise I have) as:

_____

_____

My current job/position is:

_____

_____

I am with the _____ organization.

How well does your professional dream fit with current reality?

| 1 | 2 | 3 | 4 | 5 | 6 | 7 | 8 | 9 | 10 |
|---|---|---|---|---|---|---|---|---|---|
| (Bad fit!) | | | | | | | | (Great fit!) | |

Your field?

| 1 | 2 | 3 | 4 | 5 | 6 | 7 | 8 | 9 | 10 |
|---|---|---|---|---|---|---|---|---|---|
| (Bad fit!) | | | | | | | | (Great fit!) | |

Your position?

| 1 | 2 | 3 | 4 | 5 | 6 | 7 | 8 | 9 | 10 |
|---|---|---|---|---|---|---|---|---|---|
| (Bad fit!) | | | | | | | | | (Great fit!) |

Your organization?

| 1 | 2 | 3 | 4 | 5 | 6 | 7 | 8 | 9 | 10 |
|---|---|---|---|---|---|---|---|---|---|
| (Bad fit!) | | | | | | | | | (Great fit!) |

Can you see where you need to start focusing your thinking/planning?

## Career Change Questions

Another tool to help you in the process of reassessing your career is called the *Thirty Questions to Ask Before a Career Change*. These questions can help you sort through where you have been, where you are, and where you want to go in your career at this point in your life.

THIRTY QUESTIONS TO ASK BEFORE A CAREER CHANGE

(Note: Not every question is expected to help in every situation. This is simply a checklist to help you keep from overlooking obvious questions. You will also want to add your own questions as appropriate.)

1. What do I see as the major advantages of this career change? (Make a list)

2. Why am I thinking of this change? What is my real motive?

3. What is the real price or loss that comes with this change? (Make a list)

4. What real "bones do I have to pick" with my present work situation? (Make a list). Which of these may be eliminated if I talk with my boss?

5. Is this the right time for a move?

6. In my new position do I want to put primary emphasis on the relationships I will have, the security the new position will bring, or the challenge of the position?

7. Where do I see myself in five to ten years? What is my overall career path? Does this change represent a step in the "right" direction for my longer range plans?

8. What do my closest friends (three to five) advise about the possible change? My spouse? My mentor?

9. What does my pastor say about the change?

10. How will the change affect the following areas:

    My spiritual development?
    My physical development?
    My personal development?
    My family/marriage relationship?
    My social life?
    My profession/career life?
    My financial situation?

11. If I could do anything, if I had all of the time, money, education, staff, etc.—and if God said He didn't care what I did—and I knew I couldn't fail, what would I do?

12. If I had all of the money I needed, would I still make this change?

13. If the doctor told me I had at most five years to live, what would I do then?

14. What needs do I see that make me want to weep, explode with anger, lie awake at night? Should I do something about them in my next work change?

15. What do I believe in enough to "give my life for" if necessary? In what ways can I work in support of this area?

16. What three to ten things would I most like to "do" in my work? What do I feel best at and enjoy the most?

17. In what areas would I most like to grow personally and develop my full potential? Which opportunity offers me the most potential for growth in these areas?

18. What is really holding me back in my professional life? If these could be overcome, what would I do?

19. With what person(s) would I most like to work?

20. What would I most like my epitaph to say? How would this career change affect the totality of my life work?

21. If I had all of the skills to handle any position in the world,

what position would I most like to have?

22. How much money would I honestly like to make a year? Why?

23. At what age do I plan to retire? Why? What ten things do I want to do before then?

24. What accomplishments am I most proud of at this point in my life? How would these kinds of accomplishments be possible in my new position? More of a possibility or less than my current position?

25. Have I given myself at least twenty-four hours to pray and let this decision settle in my mind?

26. Is the pressure and tension at my present situation temporary or a constant long-term problem?

27. Which position will make the most difference fifty years from today?

28. What questions are lingering in my mind that should be asked before I make a final decision?

29. What facts should I really see before I make the final decision?

30. Do I have "peace of mind" about a yes or no answer as I pray about it and look at the decision from God's eternal perspective?

# A Few "Rules of Thumb" to Consider When Making a Career Change

1. Be careful of the environment you choose, for it will shape you.
2. Who you work with may be a more important decision than the company, the pay, or even the job.
3. Run *to* something, not *away* from something.
4. Life is too short to work at something you don't enjoy, if you have a choice.
5. Choose work that lets you grow personally and become your best self, even though it may be a bit less secure.
6. Find work that lets you maximize your strengths and work on your weaknesses.
7. If you have an option, always choose a career that will be making

a difference fifty years from now because you worked today.

8. Every assignment you are given is preparing you for what God sees as your best possible position. Learn from each experience and write it down so you will remember it well.

9. Work on meeting needs you feel emotional about.

10. When it is God's move, the timing will be perfect.

A very frequent question I get about now is "Am I presidential?" "Do you think I have what it takes to be the president, the senior pastor, the head coach, governor?" If this is your question, turn to Appendix D and review the Presidential Profile. It will give you an objective basis on which to judge your presidential potential. You may want to ask a trusted friend or mentor to fill this out for you as well, giving you a bit more objectivity in your assessment.

## When You Get Released, Downsized, Fired!

You may find yourself in a position where you have no option but to look for a new position. You may have been fired, released, downsized. I would encourage you as much as possible to see this as good news. This may be what you've needed to free you, to find a better fit for you long-term. It may be painful for a few months or even a few years, but try as hard as you can to look at what difference having a job that really fits you—that energizes you and is consistent with your strengths—could mean to you for a lifetime of work.

Remember, you can predict a period of wobbling confidence in the middle of a situation in which you've been released or fired, based on the lack of predictability of where you go from here. If you can't predict the future, it's very difficult to be confident in moving toward that future, but the temporary wobble may be worth the eventual "perfect placement" of your talents.

Here's also where a mentor can be worth his or her weight in platinum. This is a time when it might be helpful for you to seek out your mentor or to find one, and to go with them through the life focus chart, through the career questions, and seek their counsel in terms of what steps to take next.

## Define Success for Yourself

What is success? There is no common understanding of success in this world today, no common definition. Success to one person is very different than success to another. There is no absolute standard. If you ask fifty people, you'll get fifty different definitions, and you'll likely end up very confused. You basically need to define success for yourself, in a way that makes sense to you.

Consider the following definition:

> Success is the feeling you get when you reach the goals you've set, or solved the problems you've committed to solving.

If you accept this definition even in a year of unemployment, you can have a successful year if your goal is to interview five companies and eliminate four of them. If the problem you're trying to solve is to think through how to get yourself out of the company you're in and you finally do it, you have succeeded. Even though the next year you may want to set goals in terms of income or possessions or some other way to define your success, this year it may be simply taking the next steps in a blurring, rough, uncertain terrain called midlife.

## Are You Feeling Time Pressure?

Do you ever get the feeling that comes with being pressured by time, the feeling of being discouraged, overwhelmed, like everything is pressing in on you and you have no time left? Do you ever get the feeling that you're living from day to day, from hand to mouth, from emergency to emergency, and from season to season?

The following seven perspectives on time will be helpful to you as you struggle to keep a balanced perspective of time and, hopefully, it will be a way for you to help other young leaders who look to you for leadership.

ONE YEAR:

> "A man tends to overestimate what he can do in one year . . . "
> Dr. Ted W. Engstrom

Frequently one of the things that causes time pressure is that you don't have a track record. You've never done what you're planning to do. Therefore, you tend to set unrealistically high goals. If you're taking on a new assignment, set lower goals for the first year until you get some track record which allows you to be more realistic. Typically, if you set a two-year goal to accomplish what you had hoped to accomplish in one year, you'll find it turns out to be much more realistic.

## THREE YEARS:

It takes three years to get any major project "off the ground."

The first day you assume responsibility for a given area, it will begin to reflect your leadership. But, before it gets to the point where you feel it's "going your way," it will take three years.

The first year tends to be a year of orientation. You're getting the feel of what the key variables are, who the people are, and what the roadblocks are.

The second year you are beginning to try things that you think will probably be the solution. You are prototyping what you think will work, revising it.

At two-plus years I've often gotten the feeling that it will never work. But, at about three years, it will either really start to be successful, or it will never be successful. Why this rule of thumb works, I don't know. But I've talked to many major developers and they all agree—it takes three years.

## FIVE YEARS:

"A man tends to overestimate what he can do in one year . . .
and underestimate what he can do in five."
Dr. Ted W. Engstrom

Progress is typically a function of time, energy, and money. The more money you have, the less time it will take, and the less energy or people. If you're limited on money and people, it's going to take a lot of time.

Another thing to realize is that most progress is not linear. Results in any area don't start and go up and up and up in a straight line. They tend to be slow in the first year or two or three, and then grow faster and faster in the later years. At the end of five years (in most projects), you'll find that much more progress has been made than you would have imagined when you started.

## TEN YEARS:

Plan to peak in ten years.

Plan your life so that ten years from today you will be at your peak in life. You'll look the best, feel the best, be more effective than you've ever been. It will be the premier year of your life. But every year on your birthday, stretch it out one year, so that when you're forty, you're just getting ready to be fifty. And when you're fifty, you're just getting ready to be sixty, and so on. This keeps you in a position of being a lifelong student. You never get to the point where you've "arrived." It gives you a future orientation rather than feeling as if your best years are in the past.

THIRTY YEARS:

A person cannot comprehend what can happen in thirty years.

Imagine ten years ago. Think of how far you have come, how different life has become during the past ten years. Now, think how far you've come in thirty years. If you're a growing person, thirty years from now would be harder to comprehend than being thirty years younger and imagining what your life would be like today.

500 YEARS:

Have a 500-year dream!

If 500 years from now humans are still on the earth, what difference will your life have made? Have a dream of what difference your life will make in 500 years. As a parent, of course, our lives make that kind of difference through our children, and their children, and their children. But ask yourself, "What will I leave that will make a difference in 500 years?"

ETERNITY:

"And time shall be no more."

There will come a time when God will step into history and decree that time shall be no more. It seems that one of the reasons God gives us prayer is to force us to an eternal perspective of time. The minute our knee touches the carpet, the reality strikes us that we are in eternity, not just time. Someday the pressures we feel or the deadlines we face will not even exist.

One of my favorite reflections is that five minutes of eternity will balance all the scales of our earthly existence. Every injustice or act of cruelty we suffer here on earth will be balanced by five minutes in the splendor of heaven or the horrors of hell. It is critical to see our time pressures on earth in light of eternity.

Action steps if you're feeling time pressure:

1. Ask, "What can I stop altogether . . . Postpone . . . Delay?"

2. Ask, "Can adding money or people reduce the time required?"

3. Take a 1, 3, 5, 10, 30, 500-year, eternal look at your situations.

As you learn to deal more effectively with time pressures, please pass along these seven perspectives to young friends, your children, and their children, and their children, and their children . . . for 500 years!

("Are You Feeling Time Pressure?" Article first printed in *Christian Management* Report, Vol. 10/No. 4, June/July 1986)

---

### Heart Probe:

You need to define your dreams. What do you want from the future?

What specific insights did you get in each of the six dream/career defining steps?

---

# THE MIDLIFE MAP

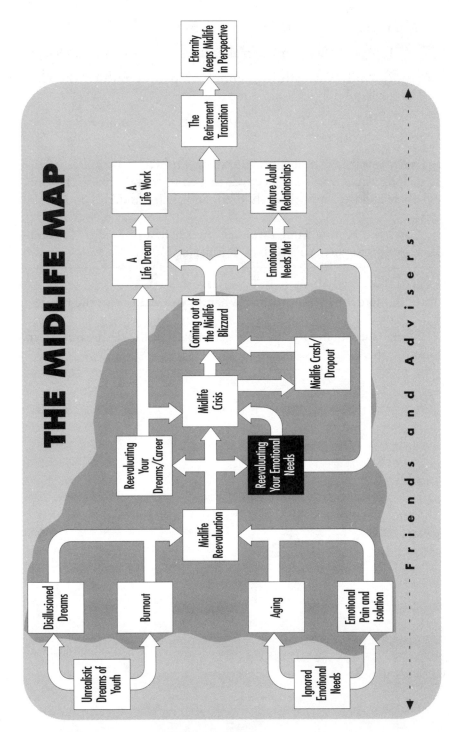

Unrealistic Dreams of Youth

Disillusioned Dreams

Burnout

Midlife Reevaluation

Reevaluating Your Dreams/Career

Reevaluating Your Emotional Needs

Midlife Crisis

Coming out of the Midlife Blizzard

Midlife Crash/Dropout

A Life Dream

A Life Work

The Retirement Transition

Emotional Needs Met

Mature Adult Relationships

Eternity Keeps Midlife in Perspective

Aging

Emotional Pain and Isolation

Ignored Emotional Needs

- - - - Friends and Advisers - - - -

© Bobb Biehl 1993

# Map Point 10: Reevaluating Your Emotional Needs

*We must identify our unmet emotional needs and develop new ways of relating to others to get these emotional needs met.*

It's time to get specific. It's time to move from a blizzard of needs and thoughts and feelings and emotions, to one (or maybe two or three) of eight emotional needs that you have in life.

One of the primary advantages and strengths of this book is to help you move from hundreds of pieces, questions, options, or concerns in your mind, to a very few, specific targets. This is one of those times. You may feel you have hundreds of emotional needs which need to be met by people. But the bottom line is that you're going to find that you need one thing more than anything else from people, and maybe two to three things more than most people do, or that are very important to you. But you don't need hundreds of things from people.

Once you can focus your attention on these two or three things and get very definitive as to what you need from your mate, your friends, your mentors, then and only then can you begin learning new ways to relate to people in order to meet these needs more effectively.

The people close to you, who want to meet your needs, cannot read your mind and heart. You have to tell them at some point, "This is specifically what I need from you."

## What Emotional Needs Do You Have That Must Be Met by Others?

Take just a minute right now and rate these on a scale of one to ten in your own life. How important is love to you in your midlife years?

How important has love been to you over the years? A word of caution: I'm not asking you to rate how important you think the concept of love is, nor how important it is to you on some absolute scale. What I'm asking you to do here is to rate how much you need love from other people, on a scale of one to ten. If you desperately need other people to love you, that's a ten.

Put an N (Need) on a scale of one to ten to indicate how important each need is to you. Put an A (Actually receive) to indicate how much this need is actually met today in your life. For example, if you rate "To Be Loved" a level nine need in your life but you feel it is only met at level three, your chart would look like this:

1   2   3   4   5   6   7   8   9   10
         A                       N

The greater the distance between A and N (when A is to the left of N) the greater the feeling of pain since the need is not being met.

When A is to the right of N you are in great shape.

When A and N are about the same level you are OK.

To Be Loved
1   2   3   4   5   6   7   8   9   10

To Make a Significant Difference
1   2   3   4   5   6   7   8   9   10

To Be Admired
1   2   3   4   5   6   7   8   9   10

To Be Recognized
1   2   3   4   5   6   7   8   9   10

To Be Appreciated
1   2   3   4   5   6   7   8   9   10

To Be Secure
1   2   3   4   5   6   7   8   9   10

To Be Respected
1   2   3   4   5   6   7   8   9   10

To Be Accepted
　　　　　1　2　3　4　5　6　7　8　9　10


What you are really after here is how much you need these things from other people, emotionally. If all of your emotions keep seeking love from other people because you haven't had enough true, unconditional love in the past, then you need love at a "ten level." But if you've had a lot of love in the past, and you say love is very important to me as a concept, I like having love, but I already have plenty of love in my life, you may rate love at a 1 or 2.

Give each of these an A and N rating, and let this list help define the unmet emotional need in your life that you need to either find out how to meet, or it will become the time bomb that leads to a lot of turbulence in your midlife years.

An interesting observation is that when the emotional need you need the very most of the eight, has been met, you feel very sexy, young, and attractive. When that need is unmet, you feel very old and unattractive. If your mate meets the need that you have for respect or love or admiration, then you're OK. But if your mate does not, or used to and doesn't anymore, then you feel old when you're with your mate, and you feel young when you're with another person who meets that need for respect, significance, acceptance, etc.

Sexuality is not just physical. As a matter of fact, from my perspective, it's not primarily physical. Attractiveness is primarily emotional. For us to feel sexually attracted to a person, he or she has to represent the possibility of that person meeting an emotional need that we have, or we do not find them attractive.

Winifred Gallagher, in his article, "Midlife Myths" (May 1993, *The Atlantic Monthly*, 60–66) referenced several studies on the midlife phenomenon. In his study of sexuality John McKinlay found that only 2 percent of the 1,700 middle-aged and older men reported having more than one current sexual partner. This figure, vastly lower than the usual guesstimates, challenges the stereotype of the bored middle-aged philanderer. Moreover, although McKinlay recorded steady declines in the men's sexual activity, from lusty thoughts to erections, he found no decrease in their sexual satisfaction, a phenomenon Gilbert Brim calls "a triumph of the adaptation of aspirations to realities." Equivalent data about women have not been gathered, but McKinlay's findings complement other surveys that show that aging has little impact on people's enjoyment of sex.

"People and their doctors," McKinlay says, "should distinguish between sexual problems caused by aging and those caused by things that often get lumped with it, such as poor health, weight gain, lack of exercise, and the use of nicotine or too much alcohol." Compared with a healthy nonsmoking peer, for example, a smoker who has heart disease has a sevenfold greater risk of impotence. Psychological fitness too plays a vital role. A man may think his primary problem is impotence caused by age when in fact his sexual trouble is a symptom of a very treatable depression. "We must not resort to biological reductionism, which is what women have been struggling against," McKinlay says.

## Vulnerability

Your point of greatest need is the point of your greatest vulnerability in ignoring moral, legal, and ethical boundaries. Here is where there is frequently an almost irresistible level of temptation to start moving into a family-leaving, a divorce-creating illicit affair. It is critical to learn how to get these needs met before they become so great that you seek relationships outside the marriage to satisfy them. If you don't work this out with your spouse, friends, and mentors, you'll find yourself working it out in illicit relationships. So it is very much worth your time, energy, and money to develop the ability to move beyond social skills and into relational comfort.

You need to be brutally honest with yourself, your mate, and with your mate's needs, so that you can learn to relate and move toward met needs and resolved relationships. If you are able to relate to your mate and friends in a way that gets these clearly identified needs met, you are on the right path to avoid a midlife crisis.

## Masks Make You Feel Safe—But Keep Your Needs From Being Met!

If you are wearing a mask of "everything is OK, you can't hurt me, I don't need you, I'm self-sufficient, I don't need anything from you," that's covering what you've just identified as a very real emotional need. Then for you to take off the mask and really let down your guard and tell someone, "I really need this from you or from people," is going to take an environment of unconditional love. If you don't feel that you're loved unconditionally, it's going to be extremely difficult for you to admit to that person with whom you are relating that you have this need.

Think through, in your own mind, who loves you without conditions, someone you could go to and say, "I feel that of all the people I know, you're one of the people who loves me the most unconditionally, and I would like to share with you some of my insights about myself, and I would like to be able to discuss them with you." Just letting another human being know rather precisely what you need would be a very positive step in your relational development.

## Socially Skilled and Relationally Unskilled

Many people are "socially skilled and relationally uncomfortable." They relate public self to public self very smoothly. They're comfortable at any party, they're comfortable at any athletic event, talking about sports, weather, playing games, keeping things on the surface. They are the kind of people everyone likes because they are socially skilled.

But when it comes to getting below the surface into the private self and then later into the personal self or into an intimate conversation where relationships develop, they've never let people beyond the mask. If this is you, be aware of the fact that it is going to be very difficult for you, but your heart is crying out for a relationship where you can move beyond the mask and into a more personal level/intimate conversation and share what's actually going on in the depths of your heart.

## The Needs of Those Around You

At the same time, particularly in relating to your mate and other close friends, it is also very important that you know what others need from you, so that it isn't just a one-way street. As needy as you are at the moment, it's important that you get these needs met in a very positive way so that it doesn't end up leading to a midlife crisis where you say, "Regardless of the consequences to my mate, my family, my friends, I'm going to seek a relationship in which these needs will be met."

## Heart Probe:

What are your needs, specifically?

Who do you trust enough to let them know how much you need what you need?

What price are you willing to pay to expose a part of what those needs are in your heart to a person to whom you want to relate to avoid a midlife crisis?

# THE MIDLIFE MAP

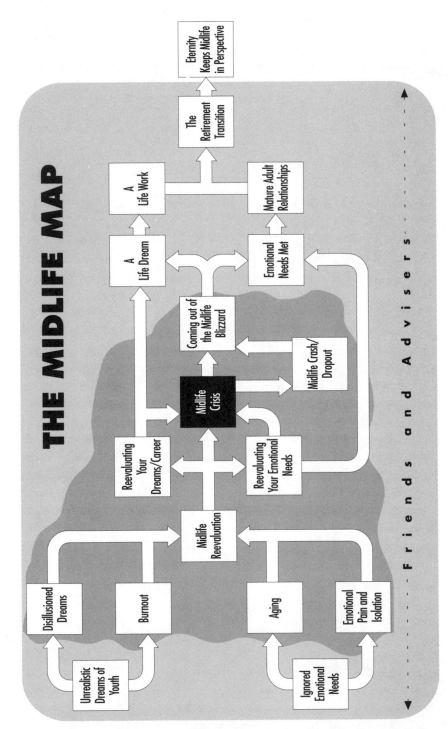

Eternity Keeps Midlife in Perspective

The Retirement Transition

A Life Work

A Life Dream

Coming out of the Midlife Blizzard

Mature Adult Relationships

Emotional Needs Met

Reevaluating Your Dreams/Career

Midlife Crisis

Midlife Crash/ Dropout

Reevaluating Your Emotional Needs

Midlife Reevaluation

Disillusioned Dreams

Burnout

Aging

Emotional Pain and Isolation

Unrealistic Dreams of Youth

Ignored Emotional Needs

- - - - Friends and Advisers - - - - - -

© Bobb Biehl 1993

# Map Point 11: Midlife Crisis

*Midlife crisis happens when we say, "Regardless of the consequences, I will have what or who I need. Regardless of the costs to me, my family, my reputation, or my future, I will pursue my dream, or I will have my emotional needs met."*

The key words here are "regardless of the cost." If you cannot define a career path or a dream that inspire you, and if you can't find a way to get your emotional needs met by learning new relational skills, the blizzard gets deeper and denser and darker. All of your emotions start crying out, *I'll never reach my dream. I don't know where I'm going. I'll never have my emotional needs met. I'm going to die here. I'm trapped. I'm alone. I'm hurting. And whatever the cost, regardless of the consequences, I will get out of this.*

Accompanying the blizzard there is typically a profound sadness, a grieving for the loss of your fantasies and your illusions—illusions that your dreams were real, and fantasies that you were connecting with people, or that your needs would someday be met if your dreams could be reached.

A special note to the person working with someone at this point in the blizzard. The person may have what seems like a normal life: a house, a car, children, a job. But the death of a dream is suffocating. He/she may have a lot of casual friends, but no one that hears the loneliness of soul. What seems to be a "Leave It to Beaver" environment to the person who looks on from the outside can be a terrifying, lonely, suffocating, drowning experience for the person in the midlife crisis.

## Extreme Vulnerability to a Person Who Connects to Your Needs

Sometimes, in the middle of your panic that your emotional needs will never be met, that your dreams are not real, and that the future is blurry, a new person comes into your life who meets your dominant emotional need or who believes in your dream, and he or she becomes a very energizing and exciting person. Anyone who doesn't believe in your dreams, who doesn't meet your needs, feels like a downer by comparison.

## Guilty with Gusto

The sheer release of finding a person who can restore any part of your dream or meet your felt needs, is so exciting that you may embrace the relationship with gusto in spite of the guilt you probably feel. There is this illusion that all your needs will be met if you could just have a relationship with this person. Things would be back to normal. I would feel alive again. I'd feel young again. I'd feel like there was hope again. I'd feel sexy and attractive and energized. Suddenly (but temporarily), you no longer feel burned out, you're not aging as fast, your needs are being met. Here, at last, you think, is someone who believes in your dreams and who will for the rest of your life!

In all candor, some second marriages actually work emotionally far better than the first marriage. I'd like to tell you that when the mate leaves the husband or wife of their youth and gets married to someone else, it never works out. The reality is that often it *does* work out. Often it's far better than it was before at an emotional level. Not at a spiritual level, not a moral level, but at an emotional level. The second mate may be far easier to live with than the first mate was. That is true even in the Christian community.

Right here it may be very, very difficult for you in your pain to remember both time and eternity, to think about your spouse, your friends, your mentors. The whole exterior world is intact, but inside the blizzard at Map Point 11 it feels like you have only one hope. And it's this new relationship, this new opportunity, even though it means leaving your job or leaving your family. You feel you can't face growing old in this setting. You're trapped in your job, trapped in your family, trapped without your emotional needs being met, and you can't face that—regardless of the consequences, even in eternity. Besides, eternity seems unreal at the moment because it's lost in the blizzard. You will do what you will do, regardless of the consequences in time or eternity.

Right here you tend to forget the sign on your grandmother's wall, "Only one life, 'twill soon be past, only what's done for Christ will last." And your emotions tell you, "only one life, 'twill soon be past, therefore I'd better go have some fun!"

Some people, because of a very disciplined younger life, have a tremendous amount of discipline built up, and it's a reserve that makes leaving family or leaving a job much more difficult than for other people. On the other hand, there are other people who are not so disciplined and who don't have the interior stamina to postpone gratification. They can't stand very much interior pain. They want the quick alternative, the quick fix, the easy answer.

If you have believed for years that divorce is a sin, you may be sorely tempted to begin to redefine and reexplain truth, to reinterpret the Scriptures, in order to get your needs met. Black and white, right and wrong, become gray in a gray fog. But above the clouds it's still black and white, right and wrong. Absolutes are still absolutes, regardless of how you feel at the moment.

It's important for you to get into your mind that there were absolutes when you were a child, there were absolutes when you were in junior high, high school, college, and as a young adult, and there are still absolutes. There are absolute rights and absolute wrongs. But when you're in the middle of the midlife crisis, that all seems gray to you. It's important to realize that the gray is only gray to you at the moment. There will come a day in which it is again black and white.

You can always find a counselor somewhere who will agree with you and counsel you to protect yourself, get out of the marriage, leave the job. Be careful that you aren't simply finding people to agree with your rationalizations at this stage. That's very, very easy to do.

Another way of creating a denser and denser gray, without the black and white, is to seek the company of those who allow adjusted value systems. Rationalization is the grease that allows their value system to shift smoothly. To meet your needs and retain some of the old value system, you need rationalization. It is very important that you seek the company of people who are outside the blizzard, whom you've trusted for years, who can help you say, "In this particular case you are absolutely right or you're absolutely wrong," and not agree with your gray. This is very important to you five years from now, ten years from now, as well as today, in the middle of your midlife crisis.

One day I was listening to the radio and I heard a man say,

"There's not a lonelier person on the face of the earth than the man whose world lies in shambles at his feet and he's forgotten how to pray." May I suggest that in the middle of this midlife crisis is when it would be wise for you to take some time away—as an honesty issue, not to please me, not to impress the pastor, not to do any of those things—to simply get your head clear, as clear as possible. Take a day away somewhere and try to look at this map and get beyond the blizzard, and look at both time and eternity.

*What does God say about all this? How do I want to be when I'm eighty, ninety? What do I want to face after I die?* And look at your spouse, your friends, your therapist, your mentors, and try to get some objective perspective through prayer. Pray and ask God to show you where you're right, where you're wrong, what dream He has for you, and what He has in mind to meet your emotional needs.

## Beware of Options

You need to know that at this point of extreme vulnerability on your part, it's easy to put up with a disillusioned dream and unmet emotional needs and *not* have illicit affairs—not even be tempted to—*if there are no options*. But when an option comes along, it may seem almost irresistible. In other words, you may never think of having an affair, but you've got all this pain built up in your heart. And all of a sudden the very person who you thought would never be interested in an affair with you, communicates that he's/she's having a similar pain. He/she may not be trying to seduce you, but somehow her/his pain matches your pain, and all of a sudden you're intimate in your conversations, the intimate conversation leads to sexual intimacy, and you're into an affair.

Most people who have affairs in midlife rarely intended them. The pastors I've talked with who have had affairs say, "I never ever intended to have that affair. It just happened." Other people, looking on from the outside, say, "Oh, sure, it just happened. Where's your self-control?" I'm saying, it did "just happen." They didn't set out to have an affair. They set out to help the other person, to maybe discuss their own situation a little bit, and all of a sudden they were emotionally locked into someone who met their needs at a level their mate didn't. It was never intended to be an affair. But because there was an option, the affair happened.

I guess I'm saying that if you do not want to have an affair, and you've got all this pain built up in your heart, all this frustration, all this blizzard, all this loneliness, be super careful about the relationships you allow to develop, because you're extraordinarily vulnerable to affairs at this moment in your life.

It is important to understand that affairs are emotional, not logical or physical. A pastor who has an affair with someone in the church does not sit down logically and say, "I'm going to risk this church that I pastor, I'm going to risk my reputation, risk hurting my family, because I'm going to go have an affair!" That is not a logical decision. Frankly, it is not a physical decision. Many times the person whom you are attracted to, is half as pretty or handsome as your own mate. But there is an emotional approachability that your mate does not have at the moment, and it makes you extremely vulnerable.

Of my many friends who have gotten a divorce, the single most common response when I look them in the eye and ask them, "Why did you get a divorce?" is a very common phrase. It's almost as though someone had written a script, and it goes like this, "We should never have been married in the first place. He or she has never really met my needs, has never supported my dreams." They go on to explain that they realize that this is not a theologically defensible reason for getting a divorce, and that divorce is, in fact wrong, and they had no biblical grounds for getting a divorce, but they're going to live with whatever the consequences are because they cannot stand the midlife pain.

One of the missions I have in life (please *join* me in this mission) is to help young people who want to get married, but who are not right for each other. I want to help them avoid a situation where in their midlife years they get caught in the vise of this trauma. This is the reason Cheryl and I did a series of marriage booklets called "Heart to Heart," listed in APPENDIX E. If you know young people either getting married or remarried, and you think they really need to know and understand each other better before they say the final "I do," consider giving them one of those booklets.

## How to Read the Midlife Symptoms

There are many jokes made about midlife symptoms: gold chains, open shirt collars, trading the Oldsmobile for a Corvette, developing "cool" haircuts, "cool" clothes, and generally trying to look hip.

This image is trying to say that even though your dreams are disappointed, you're going to live right now. You're not burned out, you're more energetic than you've ever been. You're not aging, you're actually looking younger these days. You've dyed your hair, you're looking and acting younger. Your emotional needs are not met, but you're going to go find a new, young thing that will meet your needs.

As you can see, a lot of the typical, visual symptoms of the midlife crisis can be traced right back to the four "triggers." Each person interprets his or her response to those "triggers" in different ways, but all are symptoms of at least the midlife reevaluation and, in many cases, of the midlife crisis.

A word of warning: There are a lot of people who simply try to change their image as part of the midlife reevaluation. They realize that they can make a few changes and it will make them more attractive to their spouse; they could make a few changes and it would help them at work or maybe make a career change. These are very healthy changes. But when you change to put on a mask of denial that you're growing older, that's a part of the midlife crisis.

---

## Heart Probe:

1. Be honest with yourself. Are you in the midlife crisis? Have you said in your heart, "Regardless of the consequences I will pursue my dream or I will have my needs met?"

2. Have you tried to get any kind of objectivity in your process? Unless you have, you have to question how honest you're willing to be with yourself. How much do you really want help? Or are you content to simply feel the pain, and blame God or other people?

3. Do you see clearly the way out of the midlife crisis? Are you trying to be as objective as you can be, trying to redefine your dreams, trying to learn to get your emotional needs met in an appropriate way? That's how you move out of a midlife crisis.

---

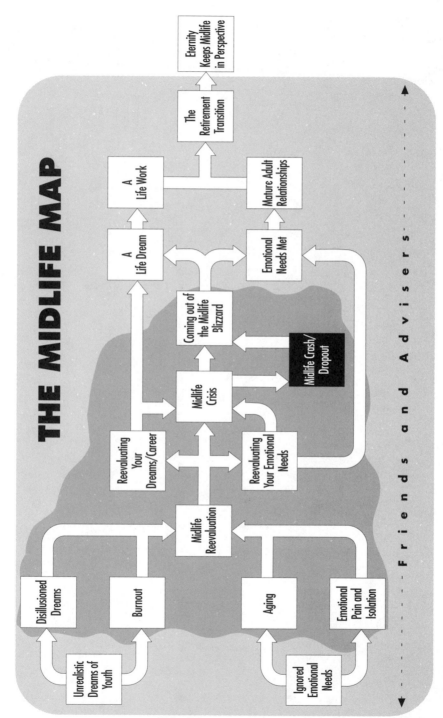

THE *MIDLIFE MAP*

Eternity Keeps Midlife in Perspective

The Retirement Transition

A Life Work

A Life Dream

Coming out of the Midlife Blizzard

Mature Adult Relationships

Emotional Needs Met

Midlife Crash/ Dropout

Midlife Crisis

Reevaluating Your Dreams/Career

Reevaluating Your Emotional Needs

Midlife Reevaluation

Disillusioned Dreams

Unrealistic Dreams of Youth

Burnout

Aging

Emotional Pain and Isolation

Ignored Emotional Needs

- - - - - Friends and Advisers - - - - -

© Bobb Biehl 1993

# Map Point 12: Midlife Crash/Dropout

*We simply get tired of trying and say, "I quit, I've had enough, I can't do this anymore. I'm out of here."*

In midlife crisis, you choose to go *to* something—something you feel is better than what you have, regardless of the consequences. In midlife dropout, you go *from* everything—not *to* something. You just drop out. In dropout you experience enormous pain without the energy or options to fix it! The word that best captures the dropout phase of the midlife blizzard is the word "crash."

## Crash: No Will to Continue, No Options—Just Crash

In the midlife dropout, there is a sense in which there are no options. You can see no options for a dream that's realistic. You feel your relational needs will never be met under any circumstance, and pretty soon your heart just gives up. Crash says, "No more! I'm not going to work anymore. I'm not going to put up with any more at home. I just quit!" It feels a little bit like being a turtle on its back. The feet move some, but there is very little forward progress.

Often a person in dropout quits a job without having a better one to go to, or burns up the savings trying to reconstruct reality. There's a sense of quiet desperation—no hope, no motivation, no discipline. It feels like you're late in the fourth quarter of a football game and the score is: Life: 150; You: 5. You have blistered feet, you're hungry, tired, and still expected to give the game of life "the old college try." It feels like the motorboat has lots of anchors but no motor, and it's beginning to sink. And there's a sense of being simply lost in the darkness of a deep, dark emotional hole.

As you're reading this, if you're in a midlife dropout phase, I imagine that this doesn't sound to you like an exaggeration. It is simply a description. But the person who is trying to help you likely thinks this must be an exaggeration, that it can't be that bad.

## Frequent Forms of Dropout

There are actually at least four kinds of dropout.

### Physical Dropout

You have headaches, lack of energy, and your body simply won't go anymore.

### Chemical Dropout: Substance Abuse

Dr. Joel Robertson, a long-time friend and a neuropharmacologist, who treats people with substance abuse problems, makes this interesting observation: "All substance abuse is, at the bottom line, self-medication." But medicating what? The severe substance abuser, in the midlife years, is a person who has so much pain that the abuse is simply trying to medicate and dull the pain that's inside.

### The Life Dropout

You experience such emotional pain that you actually run away. This person puts their thumb out and hitchhikes into oblivion, become homeless, a beach bum, a chronic prisoner, because they can't face the pain of reality and responsibility on a day-to-day basis.

### The Emotional Dropout

You simply put in the years to retirement but are never excited about your work. In extreme cases you might even end up in a mental hospital looking at the wall for the next thirty to forty years.

## Without an Adequate Answer to the Question "Why?" The Price of Change Is Always Too High

If you are in a dropout situation, it is very difficult for me to write anything that makes any sense to you. I realize that since I have not been in midlife dropout myself, it's very difficult to reach the part of you that no one has ever reached, no one has ever listened to, no one has ever understood.

But even though I don't know exactly how you feel and what you're experiencing at the moment, the depths and degree of pain you are experiencing, there are a few things I would encourage you to reflect on as you sit and watch the ocean, watch for the next car on the road, or just before you open your next bottle. Consider these things:

1. Consider the possibility of getting a pet, for example, a dog. A dog will listen while you talk. Begin to express and get things out of your heart and into words. You need to talk to someone or something, and a dog may be a good alternative.

2. Focus on some very short-term dreams. Consider a dream that may be a day or two days away, but is something that you're hoping to do, that helps you begin to dream again at some level. It feels like just getting started on anything is like climbing a wall a hundred feet high. I understand that. So this is where you take the smallest of steps. Take a step no matter how small toward having a dream of something you want to BE, DO, HAVE, or someone you want to HELP someday.

3. Regain as much objectivity as possible through the absolute truth of Scripture, through spouse, friends, therapist, or mentors who can be objective about where you are more than you can be.

4. Do anything you can to learn how to relate to people in a way that gets your emotional needs met. Seek someone out who is far worse off than you are and try to help him/her. Just the act of giving often meets some of your needs. It also restores a sense of perspective: There are actually people in this world who are far worse off than I am.

One other thought from an objective person not in the middle of the midlife blizzard anymore: a holy God and a holy heaven are still real, and He still loves you regardless of how little that feels real today. Pray this simple prayer before you go to bed:

Now I lay me down to sleep,
I pray Thee, Lord, my soul to keep.
If I should die before I wake,
I pray Thee, Lord, my soul to take.

This may sound silly to you, but I would encourage you to try it. Praying such a simple prayer can actually restore an elemental faith that God is real and does care for you, which is the absolute truth of the situation, regardless of how it feels at the moment.

---

## Heart Probe:

In midlife dropout, life feels like it is very, very hopeless.

First of all, who do you know whom you've ever trusted in your life to talk with at some level?

Second, what were your dreams a long time ago and is there any part of those that could still become real? (For example, if you used to dream of being a pro football player and now are crippled up and couldn't play sandlot ball, could you be a coach? It could be a Pop Warner team, a sandlot team, or one single kid.) Is there any part of your original dream that could still happen?

Third, consider the possibility of talking to a dog or just writing out your feelings. Sometimes just getting it onto paper, or into words, helps you see things in your own blizzard that you haven't seen before. Just to be able to say to someone or something, "Here's how I really feel," is a major release.

---

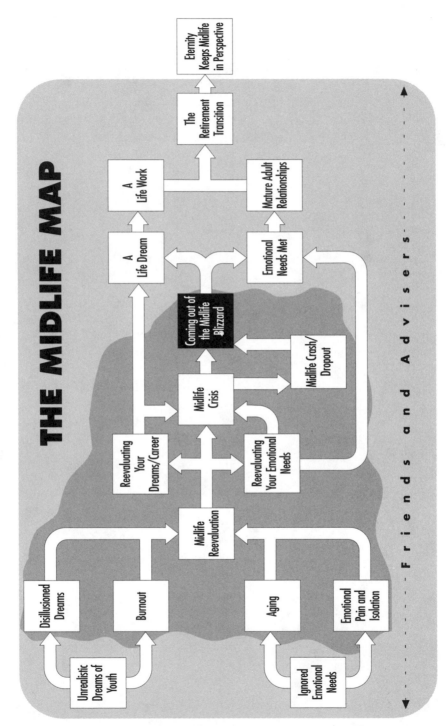

# THE MIDLIFE MAP

Eternity Keeps Midlife in Perspective

The Retirement Transition

A Life Work

A Life Dream

Mature Adult Relationships

Coming out of the Midlife Blizzard

Emotional Needs Met

Midlife Crisis

Midlife Crash/ Dropout

Reevaluating Your Dreams/Career

Reevaluating Your Emotional Needs

Midlife Reevaluation

Disillusioned Dreams

Burnout

Aging

Emotional Pain and Isolation

Unrealistic Dreams of Youth

Ignored Emotional Needs

- - - - - - F r i e n d s   a n d   A d v i s e r s - - - - - - - -

© Bobb Biehl 1993

# Map Point 13: Coming Out of the Midlife Blizzard

*Often it takes three to ten years, to regain a sense of life balance after a midlife crisis or crash.*

Midlife is a blizzard of questions surrounding two issues: one is a dream that is worthy of my life's time, energy, and resources, and the other is getting my emotional needs met. That's the essence of it. So, to come out of the midlife blizzard, you have to find some way of dealing with all these questions.

Let me suggest the following steps for a starting place:

1. Come to grips with what you believe. As Tom Skinner advised during his life, "I spent a long time trying to come to grips with my doubts, and suddenly I realized that I had better come to grips with what I believe. I have since moved from the agony of questions that I cannot answer, to the reality of answers that I cannot escape—and it's a great relief."

2. Make a list of questions about your Dream/Career, about your Emotional Needs, and about your life in general. Make an exhaustive list of every question left in your head. That list could be 100 questions, it could be 10,000 questions. Make a list of every single question that is causing your mind to blur.

3. Get a huge sheet of paper (continuous computer paper works well) and construct a framework, or grid large enough for you to write in all your questions. Write at the top "QUESTIONS I HAVE FLOATING AROUND IN MY HEAD."

Some of your questions you will see as "penny" questions, little questions you have that you think aren't that important. Some are "dollar" questions, a little more important, some "ten-dollar questions," some "hundred-dollar" questions—fairly substantial, some "thousand-dollar" and some "million-dollar" questions. Million-dollar questions are the really tough questions, the imponderable questions, the "Solomon-stumpers" questions.

## QUESTIONS I HAVE FLOATING AROUND IN MY HEAD

| Penny Questions | $1 Questions | $10 Questions | $100 Questions | $1,000 Questions | $1 Million Questions |
|---|---|---|---|---|---|
|  |  |  |  |  |  |

Make this chart as long as it needs to be to hold every single question you have anywhere in your head.

4. Now take all of your questions, no matter how many, and write them in this framework somewhere. Then read Tom Skinner's quote again.

5. Take a similar-sized paper and write across the top "WHAT I BELIEVE TODAY."

   You may want to make a rather comprehensive list broken up any way you like. Here are a few possibilities:
   - What you believed as a child
   - What you believed as a teen—which may be substantially different
   - What you believed as a young adult—which may be substantially different again
   - What you are supposed to believe today and don't
   - What other people expect you to believe but it just doesn't make sense to you
   - What you really believe today, regardless of what anyone else thinks
   - I have no idea what I believe about these things anymore, I haven't a clue

It's going to take you a few months to a few years to get out of this midlife blizzard you're in, but if you'll work on it every once in a while, an hour a day, a day here and there, some time during the week, this gives you a framework for all those pieces of confetti floating around in your mind and heart. It helps you know how to distinguish between the penny questions and the million-dollar questions, between what you believe and what you really don't believe anymore.

When you get a few minutes to a few hours with a friend or confidant, you now have a few prioritized questions and discussion points upon which you can focus. Your conversations are not a fast and furious blizzard of questions alternating between penny questions and million-dollar questions.

My friend, just the passage of time will not bring you out of the midlife blizzard. You can be seventy-five years old and still wrestling with the issues of life: something to believe, something to dream about, finding a friend who is sensitive to meet your emotional needs. But if you'll be patient and simply work at it step by step, over time your head and your heart will clear up.

When I came out of my midlife years, I had days when I was clear and days when I was still back in the fog. I would go along for a few days when I was still extremely fogged over, and then I would have a day that was just crystal clear. And I would think, "Oh, now I'm over it, now I'm past the blizzard," and three days later it would hit me again. Don't be discouraged if you have intermittent days when things still seem in a blizzard as you move from Map Point 13 to Map Point 14 and 16. But if you'll just hang tight and keep working at it, you will come out of it as thousands and millions have before you. THERE IS HOPE!

## A Sounding-Board Friend

One of the most fundamental needs you have in coming out of your midlife blizzard is a sounding-board friend. Ask yourself this question: "Of all the people I know, who is the one person I trust the most for her/his objectivity, her/his wisdom, her/his care for me, her/his ability to help me sort things out?"

This can be a person without a high school education, or it can be a Ph.D. counselor. It can be an uncle or an aunt who lives in a distant state, or a brother or sister that lives five miles from you. It can be a college friend, it could be a buddy you grew up with, a friend from high school. It might be a youth worker whom you trusted a lot, or it could be a current or former pastor.

But find this one person and make an appointment with him or her. Say you've got a list of questions you need to discuss with a trusted friend, and would he/she be willing to spend some time with you? Go over your questions and your beliefs with this trusted friend. And ask the friend, as an objective sounding board, to help you begin to sort out the pieces.

## Some Practical Steps to Speed Up the Process

Because this is such an important step in the midlife map, please consider the following specific "Midlife Blizzard Ejector" options. You certainly do not need to do them all. But consider each and see which might appeal to you or be the most helpful at the moment as you are coming out of the midlife blizzard.

1. Fill out the EMOTIONAL BALANCE CHART (see APPENDIX A)

    The emotional balance chart gives you an objective framework for studying what thoughts and feelings help you be positive, and which ones lead to negative thinking.

2. Construct a LIFELONG FRIENDS LIST.

    This is simply an exhaustive list of all the people you know and would like to be friends with for the rest of your life.

    Take your Christmas card list and add to it anyone you can think of. Not everyone on your Christmas list may be on your lifelong friends list, but make a list of all the people—not only where you live but anywhere in the world—who are your friends for life.

    What this list does is document Map Point 1 on the midlife map. The fact is, you do have friends even though some may live at a distance and you haven't talked to them for a year or more. And it gives an objective way to see how many people care whether you live or die.

3. Make a POSITIVE PROGRESS LIST.

    Make a list of all the things you've done right in life. (You may want to add to the top of the list these words, "Things God has used me to do in life.") This has been one of the most helpful exercises I've gone through in my adult life. In a midlife reevaluation, or midlife crisis, or midlife dropout, it's easy to look at all of our failures and all the things we didn't do right and get discouraged and negative.

Go back to as far as you can remember as a child and write out all the things that you've done right. These may not be things that would be worthy of the evening news broadcast. But they are things that you feel you've done right, lessons you've learned, times when you showed integrity, character, etc. Make a list of all of the progress you've made physically, socially, financially, spiritually, professionally, etc. List milestones like family vacations you've taken, courses you've taken, awards you've received, people you've helped, etc. Anything that you feel is positive progress.

Then, whenever you get discouraged, get out this list and review it. About once every three months update it. I have mine in the laptop computer I carry with me all the time. And it's very easy for me, no matter where I am, to stop and say, "What has happened in the last month or so that's been positive progress or a milestone?" And then I make a note of it. So, after ten years, I have a long list of things I feel I've done right. And I keep adding things over the years.

By the way, the positive progress list can also be negative things that have happened to you from which you feel you've learned a valuable life lesson, and that now becomes a positive progress point in life.

4. Find a MENTOR for objectivity.

Who are the few people—with whom you have a lifelong relationship, who want to see you do well, who have more experience than you in some area—who you could ask to be one of your life mentors?

If you do not feel confident in finding a mentor, you might want to read, Mentoring: How to Find One and How to Become One. (See APPENDIX E)

5. Reread the "ARE YOU FEELING TIME PRESSURE" article in chapter 9 of this book, and decide that you'll plan to peak in ten years. Then, write out what you want life to be like ten years from now.

6. THINK OF YOUR PARENTS BY THEIR FIRST NAMES (when you see them, call them Mom and Dad or whatever you normally call them). Even if they've passed away, from now on whenever you think of your parents in your mind, call them by their first names.

What this does is adjust your expectation of what is realistic to expect from them, and it lets you see them adult to adult, instead of adult to child. As a part of the midlife maturing process, this is often helpful.

7. GIVE YOURSELF PERMISSION NOT TO BE PERFECT, allow yourself time to sort these things out.

This may not sound like a very specific thing, but it is very important that you give yourself the permission not to be perfect. You're working on it and you're moving in the right direction. Don't get discouraged at this point.

8. DON'T BE DISCOURAGED when you find yourself in a foggy day again. You may well have blue-sky days and cloudy days, intermittently, for several months, if not several years.

9. Consider getting a NEW AUDIENCE. Who is it that you turn to when trying to decide how you're doing in life? With whom do you compare yourself? These people are your audience. These are the people who, at least in your mind, are watching your behavior and either applauding or booing.

Consider that there may be a different person or group of people with whom you should be associating. W. Clement Stone once said, "Be careful of the friends you choose, for in fact you will become like them." Decide where you want to be in ten years, and plan to begin making friends with the people you'd like to have as friends ten years from now—if, in fact, they are different from who your friends are today.

10. KNEEL AND PRAY ONCE A DAY.

This may sound simple, silly, or even hypocritical to you as you're coming out of your midlife blizzard. But the very fact that you are kneeling and praying reminds you, in a physical as well as an emotional way, that eternity and God are still very real. It doesn't matter what you say; you can confess to God, you can praise God, you can ask God questions, you can talk to God, you can discuss some of your questions with God—anything at all. And even though it may feel like there's no answer, just keep doing it. You're going to find that it adds a dimension of perspective and objectivity and truth and reality to coming out of your midlife blizzard that's very helpful.

# A New "Normal"

Perhaps one of the more helpful bits of advice I've ever heard from a counselor was the one who was counseling a young couple who had just had their third child. The husband, in a rather exasperated tone, pleaded, "Doctor, when are things ever going to get back to normal? When we had two children, if one cried, one of us could pick up the one, and if the other one cried, the other could pick it up. Now we have a third. Who picks up the third? Everything takes longer. We get less sleep, etc."

The doctor very wisely responded, "What you have to do is realize that this is the new normal. It now takes twenty minutes to get ready, not fifteen. You will get less sleep than you did. There will be more bills with three than two. This is the new normal."

My point here is that there is a new normal when you're forty or fifty years old compared to when you were fifteen or twenty. But that's not all bad. Listen to Ron Kessler.

> Although there are plenty of exceptions, "the data show that middle age is the very best time in life," says Ronald Kessler, a sociologist and MIDMAC fellow who is a program director in the survey research center of the University of Michigan's Institute for Social Research. "When looking at the total U.S. population, the best year is fifty. You don't have to deal with the aches and pains of old age or the anxieties of youth: Is anyone going to love me? Will I ever get my career off the ground? Rates of general distress are low—the incidences of depression and anxiety fall at about thirty-five and don't climb again until the late sixties. You're healthy. You're productive. You have enough money to do some of the things you like to do. You've come to terms with your relationships, and the chance of divorce is very low. Midlife is the 'it' you've been working toward. You can turn your attention toward being rather than becoming."

> If youth's theme is potential, midlife's is reality: childhood fantasies are past, the fond remembrances of age are yet to be, and the focus is on coming to terms with the finite resources of the here and now. The overwhelming majority of people, surveys show, accomplish this developmental task, as psychologists put it, through a long, gentle process—not an acute, painful crisis. Over time the college

belle or the high school athlete leans less on physical assets, the middle manager's horizons broaden beyond the corner office, and men and women fortunate enough to have significant others regard the rigors of courtship with indulgent smiles. In relying on brains and skill more than beauty and brawn, diffusing competitive urges to include the tennis court or a community fund-raising project, and valuing long-term friendship and domestic pleasures over iffy ecstasies, these people have not betrayed their youthful goals but traded them in for more practical ones that bring previously unsuspected satisfaction. Ronald Kessler says, "The question to ask the middle-aged person isn't just *What has happened to you?* but also *How has your experience changed your thinking?*" ("Midlife Myths" by Winifred Gallagher, May 1993, *The Atlantic Monthly*, 51–53)

## Heart Probe:

What are your lingering questions?

What do you really believe?

Who do you really trust the very most to be an objective sounding board for you at this point in your life?

How committed are you to getting out of the midlife blizzard? Are you ready to spend the time, energy, and resources it takes? Will you take the practical steps necessary to once and for all escape the blizzard and define your new dream, form resolved, mature, adult relationships, and move on into an exciting *new normal?*

Congratulations! You're almost there!

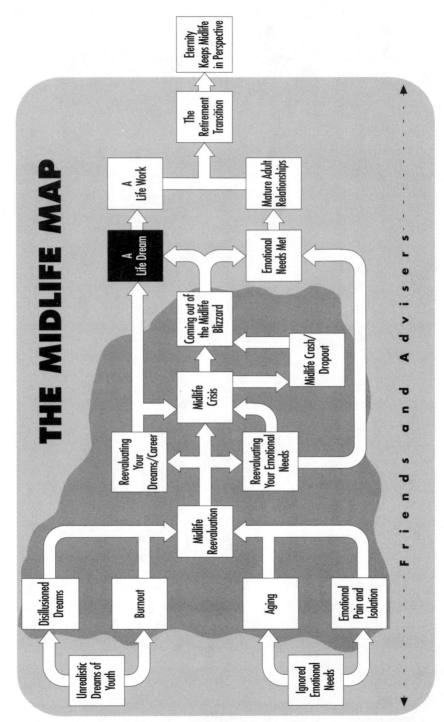

# THE MIDLIFE MAP

Eternity Keeps Midlife in Perspective

The Retirement Transition

A Life Work

A Life Dream

Coming out of the Midlife Blizzard

Midlife Crisis

Reevaluating Your Dreams/Career

Midlife Crash/Dropout

Reevaluating Your Emotional Needs

Emotional Needs Met

Mature Adult Relationships

Midlife Reevaluation

Disillusioned Dreams

Burnout

Aging

Emotional Pain and Isolation

Unrealistic Dreams of Youth

Ignored Emotional Needs

Friends and Advisers

© Bobb Biehl 1993

# Map Point 14: A Life Dream

This is where we define our new or revised LIFE DREAMS.

DREAMS MAKE A DAILY DIFFERENCE
Without dreams
a person flops out of bed in the morning,
drifts through the day,
and jumps into bed at night,
frustrated at the lack of significant life progress.

With dreams
a person jumps out of bed in the morning,
focuses on high priority next steps,
and flops into bed at night,
thankful for any bit of progress towards the dream.

To avoid a midlife crisis or dropout or the frustration of coming out of the midlife blizzard, one of the two most fundamental things you can possibly do is to define a new or revised dream. A "LIFE DREAM" answers the question, "What can I do to make the most significant difference in my lifetime?"

# Your Life Dream: Six Key Considerations

*A Life Dream Can Be a Be, Do, Have, or Help Dream*
Your life dream can encompass what you wish to become, what you wish to achieve, what you wish to possess, or who you wish to help. But whatever it is, it is about making a significant difference in the world. How will the world be a different place because you lived?

Once you define your life dream, you may find it to be very different from what you had imagined at age twenty, or even at forty!

*A Life Dream Can Be a Revision of a Young, Unrealistic Dream*
Dreams can be a modification, a refinement, or an improvement of an old and faded dream. You may have dreamed of playing pro football, but today your dream is to help kids play football. You may have dreamed you'd be an opera star, and now you dream of teaching voice at a local conservatory.

Today's dream is a realistic dream based on a realistic self-assessment. Based on your strengths, your limitations, your current realities, what difference do you want your life to make between now and the day you die? That's your dream.

*Life Dreams Energize!*
Whatever it takes to sort out, define, and perfect your life dream, it is time, energy, and money well spent. The reason is that a dream is one of the main sources of natural life energy. A dream will get you out of bed in the morning, empower you on a day-to-day basis, focus your sense of destiny.

*Your Life Dream Can Also Be a Magnificent Obsession*
Your life dream can be a hidden dream, a dream that you share with no one but yourself. You do not have to be held accountable for your dreams.

Most of the dreams in the history of mankind have been hidden deep in the heart of the dreamer, inspiring, but never once spoken.

*Life Dreams Need to Be Significant Enough to Change for,*
*without Complaint*
Go for a dream for which you are willing to change, grow, get stronger, become a different person.

*A Life Dream Does Not Have to Be Putting a Man on the Moon, or
Winning the National Championship*

It can be as simple a matter as raising healthy, happy, godly children. It can be as simple as mentoring young leaders or young people in your church or neighborhood or club.

My Grandfather Donaldson was a man who had a dream his entire lifetime that 99.9 percent of the people who ever knew him did not clearly understand. But it illustrates well the point I'm trying to make here. Your dreams do not have to be earth-shaking to make a significant difference in the world. A simple, loving shoe cobbler in the small village of Mancelona, Michigan, Lee Donaldson had a dream—a life dream. His life dream was consistently reflected in his character and life endeavors.

Grandpa died when I was too young to have had many serious conversations with him. I was still of the belief that everyone lived forever. There was no rush to discuss serious matters. But, by my definition, Grandpa was eminently qualified as a person with a "life dream."

He was a man who basically ignored a wide variety of social conventions. He wore old clothes, drove old cars thirty-five miles an hour on the highway. He never sought a high position. He cried a lot when he felt love or compassion. But he had a life dream. His dream kept him energized day after day. And, night after night.

His dream helped him love everyone he met. His dream helped him confidently confront injustice as he met it. His dream gave him energy, stamina, discipline. Kept him positive even when sick. Kept him optimistic even while living without many material possessions.

He talked often of his dream—even though he wouldn't have thought to call it a life dream. His constant and energizing dream: being in heaven and hearing Jesus say to him, "Well done, Lee. You have been a good and faithful servant. Enter now into the joy of the Lord."

This life dream kept Grandpa Donaldson cleaning toilets at our local church when no one was around. It kept him reading his Bible night after night when no one noticed. It kept him giving an honest day's work for less than most considered an honest day's pay. In short, his life dream kept him focused. Kept him energized. Kept him independently motivated. Kept him disciplined. Kept him growing. Kept him cheerful and optimistic in meager life circumstances. Kept him serving people in the name of Jesus.

Grandpa had a second-grade education. He learned to read by reading the Bible. Raised seven children. Attended church to worship, not to avoid guilt. Stayed married to Cora Donaldson for over sixty years. Grandpa didn't have a dream of accomplishing some grand thing. He had no dreams of accumulated wealth. He had no records to set. But he had a dream that inspired him a lifetime. That is a life dream.

Ask yourself, "What do I believe in enough to invest my life in?" Don't be surprised if the question leads you back to things like God, taking kids to Sunday School, church, roots, family, etc. Once you answer the question, your new dream will bring a fresh energy in a major new way.

## Mentoring Is a Dream Anyone Can Have

One of the words that is misunderstood in our society is "mentoring." People quickly assume that you have to be eighty years old and teaching child protégés piano in order to be a mentor. The reality is that anyone can be a mentor, anyone who cares for someone else and has more experience that they are willing to share with that person.

In my book *Mentoring*, I define it this way: "Mentoring is a lifelong relationship in which a mentor helps a protégé realize her or his God-given potential." Consider the possibility that a part of your dream is spotting young leaders or young people who wouldn't make it in life without you, and coming alongside them as a mentor, as a person who brings an objective, caring perspective to their lives and helps them realize their God-given potential.

---

### Heart Probe:

Bottom line, what is your life dream?

What is it that energizes you to get out of bed in the morning?

What difference do you want to make sometime before you die?

What do you want to be, do, have, who do you want to help?

What difference do you want your life to make?

---

Commit your answers to paper in a few words. Get to where you know with crystal clarity the difference you want to make. That is your dream. And as that dream becomes clear, natural energy will enable you to move in that direction, helping pull you out of your midlife blizzard.

Remember, this dream can be hidden in your heart, or it can be shared with a few trusted friends, at your discretion. Either way, you'll find that it can energize you for a lifetime.

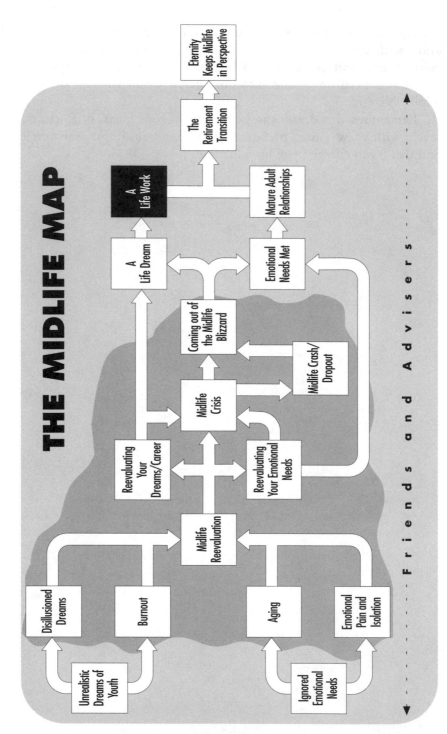

# THE MIDLIFE MAP

Eternity Keeps Midlife in Perspective

The Retirement Transition

A Life Work

A Life Dream

Mature Adult Relationships

Coming out of the Midlife Blizzard

Midlife Crisis

Midlife Crash/Dropout

Reevaluating Your Dreams/Career

Reevaluating Your Emotional Needs

Emotional Needs Met

Midlife Reevaluation

Disillusioned Dreams

Burnout

Aging

Emotional Pain and Isolation

Unrealistic Dreams of Youth

Ignored Emotional Needs

- - - - Friends and Advisers - - - -

© Bobb Biehl 1993

# Map Point 15: A Life Work

*Using the Life Work Chart, we can define our new life work in the light of our new, motivating dreams.*

In light of your life dream, what work is worthy of the rest of your life's time, energy, and money? This is a question I've asked probably hundreds of executives over the last twenty years. A lot of people, as they're coming out of the midlife blizzard, have an assumption that they should begin looking for a career change or a job change. The reality is that what you are looking for is your "life work." Your life work is what you will do for the rest of your life—to move in the direction of your life dream.

Incidentally, this is Map Point 15, not 14, because a life dream does precede a life work. You need a life dream first, and then you need a life work that helps you fulfill your dream.

## Twenties

The focus of our twenties is what we *must do* to survive. We either get a *job*, where we trade our "brains and our backs for bucks," are told what to do, and when and how to do it, or we learn a *profession* where we trade our expertise for dollars.

Actually, the twenties is the bridge between adolescence and adulthood. I have often counseled young people in their early twenties with the following words, "Use your twenties as a time to find out what you do *not* want to do." You may end up with many jobs in your twenties, each of which lasts a year or two, but if you are able to move around and find out what you do *not* want to do, you have used the decade of your twenties well.

## Thirties

Our thirties is a shift in focus from *survival* to *success* and from what we *must do* to what *we want* to do. Whether we have a *job*, such as painting houses, or a *profession*, such as being a medical doctor, by the time we are in our thirties, most likely both have become *careers*. The house painter refers to a career in "house-painting"; the doctor a career in "medicine."

The thirties is a time when we begin moving ourselves "up the ladder" to the bigger and better, more responsibility, more money, more benefits, and more things. These advances feel like emotional proof that we have passed survival and are successful.

## Forties

In our forties, we move from being primarily motivated by *success*, the feeling we experience when reaching our goals, to a focus on s*ignificance*, making a difference that will last over time. Frequently, even in our forties, we have not defined our life work. As a result, many get stuck in the success syndrome and feel that life means simply to accumulate, accumulate, and accumulate. The success syndrome stagnates, and we end up in our late forties extremely successful yet feeling insignificant—experiencing life as hollow and shallow. We conclude we may as well get all we can out of life because life gives us very little in return.

## Life Work

Many leaders I have talked to over the last ten years have concluded that they are very successful in their careers, but these careers are not necessarily what they want to do for the rest of their lives. They are seeking what I refer to as their life work.

Men and women seeking a life work often state their search in different ways: "I guess I'm just a 'jack of all trades and a master of none,'" or, "I'm still trying to figure out what I want to be when I grow up" or, "I'm not doing what I plan to do someday, but I haven't figured out what that is yet" or similar comments.

As a result of helping many executives struggle through the troubled waters of mid-to-late forties' reevaluation, I began trying to define the critical variables in determining one's life work. These men and women were looking for ways to maximize their experience and success and, at the same time, serve God and make a true difference in eternity. The best way I can help you determine if what you are doing is your life work is by defining some of the components of life work. The following are ten characteristics which will be true of your life work:

### 1. Your Single Greatest Strength

Most people (especially modest people) find defining their single greatest strength very difficult. However, this is one of the most helpful self-definition exercises I could recommend. Whatever your life work turns out to be, it will maximize your single greatest strength.

Actually everyone possesses two "single greatest strengths!" Surprisingly, this is not a contradiction. One of your single greatest strengths is a "be" strength; the other a "do" strength. Your "be" strength, you may conclude, is loyalty, honesty, faithfulness, wisdom, courage, or some other trait. On the "do" side, the strength may be communicating, conceptualizing, designing, selling, engineering, etc. Choose a strength on each side. In your single greatest strength, you will find *easy* what others find difficult or impossible.

Some teachers have suggested people should spend up to 50 percent of their time on their strength areas and 50 percent on their weak areas, trying to overcome their weaknesses. My perspective is to identify your single greatest strength and spend 95 percent of your time in that area and only 5 percent working on your growth areas.

### 2. You Love It!

When you find your life work, you will do that work even if no one ever pays you for it. I read a sign when I was twenty years old that said, "An activity is work only when you would rather be doing something else." By that definition, I retired at age thirty-four when I started Masterplanning Group. The vast majority of my time is spent consulting, and I love it so much that I would consult even if no one paid me. As a matter of fact, I find that when I am spending a day with a close friend, I often end up consulting, obviously without being paid for it.

### 3. You Never Tire of It!

You may get tired while doing your life work, but you never tire of the result. I get tired and fatigued consulting, but I never tire of the beauty I see when people begin to have clarity instead of fogginess in their eyes. I have been consulting since 1976, and, to me, every day seems new. I just never tire of it. I have told many people that consulting is my life work.

### 4. Others Affirm You in This Niche

Maybe many things done in the past just didn't seem to fit. Friends who are open and honest might say, "I don't think you will be doing this long. I don't think it is really you." However, when we find our life work, we will find our closest friends saying, "Aha! You have now found your true niche." That is one of the confirmations of finding your life work.

### 5. Adequate Income to Make a Living

Many artists would like to have painting, acting, or singing be their life work, but if you asked if they could make a living at it, they would say, "Oh, no, it's more like a hobby." In order to qualify as a life work, you must be able to make a living doing it (or be financially independent to do it without needing money).

### 6. Role Preference Consistency

Fulfillment, or rather the lack of it, is probably the single greatest buzz word for people who are trying to sort out their life work. The lack of fulfillment is the reason $500,000-per-year executives resign from corporate America and teach college for $40,000. Lack of fulfillment is the reason top executives take lower salaries at other companies offering freshness and new challenges.

In my experience, lack of fulfillment comes as a result of playing a role you are not designed to play. For example, to be fulfilled, a designer must design; a developer must develop. Otherwise, neither will feel a sense of fulfillment. (See Role Preference Inventory in APPENDIX E.)

### 7. A Significant Use of the Rest of Your Life

As you look ahead to twenty or thirty years of active service, it's critical to be able to conclude that what you are doing is the best use of your life. You must conclude that this work would be a worthy use, a noble use, a "highest good" use of your life, or you will feel your current career is not your life work.

### 8. Utilize a Proven Model

Many are successful in their careers yet do not have an ability to predict from day to day if what they are doing will work in the same way it did yesterday. It is not a proven model. In the last five years, I cannot remember a day of consulting that has been a truly bad day. Some have certainly been less effective than others, but in each, I felt I had grappled with the heart of the issue and had seen progress in the process. I have a proven model for consulting as a basis for my life work.

Another example could be a pastor preparing his sermons. Mature pastors develop a proven model for sermon preparation, and every time they get in the pulpit, they "hit the ball out of the park." However, if they don't really know how to prepare, every sermon would simply be "hit or miss." They would not have a proven model for a life work.

### 9. Life Work Maximizes Your History of Experience

The late Dr. Richard Halverson became chaplain of the Senate at age sixty-five. He remarked, "God has spent sixty-five years getting me ready for this position."

When I decided that consulting was to be my life work, I looked back, and every experience (both positive and negative) seemed to fit into place, like a thousand-piece puzzle. Consulting is an ideal way to maximize every experience I had had over my life. It maximizes my history!

Once you define your life work you too will see how God has uniquely prepared you for this work.

### 10. Life Work Feels As If "This Is Me!"

When you find your life work, you will have a sense of well-being—settledness, harmony, peace of mind—knowing that you are dealing in your primary strength. You love it; you never tire of it; others affirm you in it; you can make a living at it; it is consistent with the way God designed you; it is significant; you have a proven model; it maximizes your experience; and you are able to say with comfortable conviction, "This is me!"

Coming to clarity on the subject of your life work is typically not a quick and easy journey, but it is well worth the effort! Never stop until you are:

- In the right field,
- With the right organization, and
- In the right position.

This may require a lot of time, energy and money on your part to find just the organization that fits your talent. Here's where a mentor can give you objective assessment, perspective, and maybe even network to open doors in finding the niche that fits you for your life work.

(Used by permission from a Masterplanning Group resource called "Career Decision/LifeWork")

---

**Heart Probe:**

What is your life work?

What is it that you will do without tiring for the rest of your life?

---

Have you found your life work? If not, spend whatever time it takes at this point in your life defining what that life work will be. And when you do, there will be an "aha" in your heart. You will see why every piece of your experience in life has gotten you ready for this position. Everything will make sense at that point, because God has been building into your life a wide variety of experiences, positive and negative, to get you ready for your unique life work.

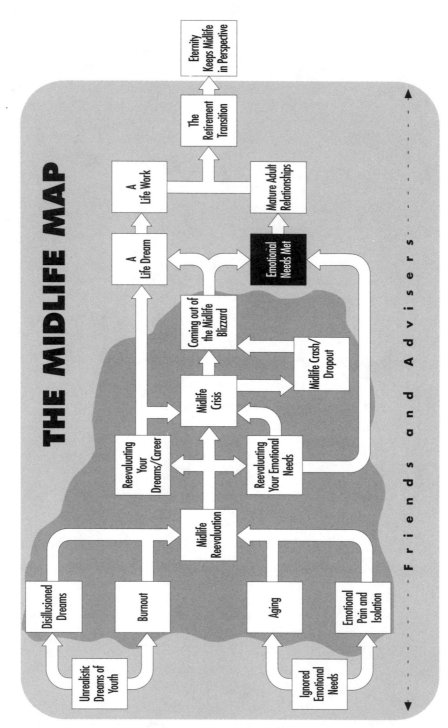

# THE *MIDLIFE MAP*

Unrealistic Dreams of Youth → Disillusioned Dreams

Burnout

Disillusioned Dreams → Midlife Reevaluation

Burnout → Midlife Reevaluation

Aging → Midlife Reevaluation

Ignored Emotional Needs → Emotional Pain and Isolation

Emotional Pain and Isolation → Midlife Reevaluation

Midlife Reevaluation → Reevaluating Your Dreams/Career

Midlife Reevaluation → Reevaluating Your Emotional Needs

Reevaluating Your Dreams/Career → Midlife Crisis

Reevaluating Your Emotional Needs → Midlife Crisis

Midlife Crisis → Coming out of the Midlife Blizzard

Midlife Crisis → Midlife Crash/Dropout

Coming out of the Midlife Blizzard → A Life Dream

A Life Dream → A Life Work

Emotional Needs Met → Mature Adult Relationships

A Life Work → The Retirement Transition

Mature Adult Relationships → The Retirement Transition

The Retirement Transition → Eternity Keeps Midlife in Perspective

- - - Friends and Advisers - - -

© Bobb Biehl 1993

# Map Point 16: Emotional Needs Met

*Once we have formed new relational skills, we discover healthy ways of relating to people who in turn meet our emotional needs.*

Once your needs are met, you are free for the first time to meet the needs of others. This is a wonderful focus in life. Find out what a person needs most and continue to give it to her/him.

You may ask, "Isn't that manipulative?" If you are meeting their needs just so you will get something in return, yes. But if you're doing it as a simple human kindness, it is not. Imagine for a minute that a close friend comes to your house. You can tell she has walked a long way and is desperately thirsty. You know that her very favorite drink on earth is ice-cold, home-made lemonade. And, you just happen to have a pitcher full in your refrigerator. Would it be manipulative to offer to go to the refrigerator and get her a cold glass of lemonade to quench her thirst? Of course not. It's simply meeting one of her obvious needs.

Starting with you children, your spouse, your parents, your siblings, the people at work, determine what the emotional need is and meet it to the best of your ability. You will find it very rewarding, indeed.

## Understanding Needs Allows Precision in Meeting Needs— Yours and Others'

It isn't until you have that specific understanding of what their needs are that you are able to meet their needs with pinpoint accuracy. Here are a few additional tips:

If you determine that your wife's insatiable need is to be loved, then she is more than likely a perfectionist and longs to hear that she's done things exactly right. As a matter of fact, she may long to hear that she's done them "perfectly." When she asks you, "How was dinner?" if it was exactly what you needed (for nourishment, energy), why not say, "It was perfect!" Later, you may want to reassure her that you would love her even if the dinner had been anything but perfect. What she really needs to hear is that she is loved without conditions! That she does not have to perform perfectly to be worthy of your love.

In the case of a husband who needs to make a significant difference, help him see the difference he's making. Let him know that you see the significant difference he is making. Help him see that because he was there, the party was different. Because he was there, the game was different. Because he was there, work was different. Tell him, in a hundred ways how his being there made a significant difference.

Relating to a person who needs to be admired, make a game out of seeing how many ways you can say, "Wow!" This person needs to hear comments such as, "Wow, how did you do that? Amazing! That was wonderful! That's incredible! How did you do that so fast?"

Always call the person who needs to be recognized by name. The person needing recognition desperately needs to hear her/his own name. Not "Hey," or "Would you mind," or even "Honey" or "Dear." Call the person needing recognition by name.

The person needing recognition does not necessarily need public recognition. Even though when you go into her/his office he/she may have, as Kay James calls it, an "I like me wall" of diplomas, trophies, and awards. Though meaningful at a given moment, such awards are given in public for public deeds (or on behalf of the public), and they fail to deeply satisfy.

What the person who needs recognition is really after is someone who will see the personal self. See how hard he/she tries, the love, the care in his/her heart. See the commitment to integrity, to quality, etc. And he/she also could very much appreciate having a pet name, a nickname, or what I call a "heart name" (a name that only you call only her/him, and only when you're alone).

For the children in your life that you care deeply about, always give them a "heart name" while they're young—a name that's very positive, that perhaps speaks to a unique strength they have, a unique character trait. Children assume that when you use that heart name, you're talking to the real them, their heart. And when they get to be teenagers you'll have direct access to their heart by simply using the heart name, whenever you are alone with them.

If your friend needs to be appreciated, what he/she longs to hear is "Good job. Great job! Job well done. Thank you. That was more than enough. You did a super job. That was incredible!"

If the person needs security, what he/she really wants to hear is that everything is under control—financially, physically, emotionally, etc. If a person you love needs a lot of security, simply tell her/him how much you're trying to help her/him be secure. Position certain things you do for her/him in light of security. For example, if you make an investment and you know that your wife is a security-oriented person, say, "Honey, by putting this thousand dollars in this special trust account, what I'm trying to do is give you more security. I want to make sure that we have our future in financial control." This person really enjoys hearing how everything is in control and under control.

If the person you care a lot about really needs respect, demands respect, tell her/him you respect who he/she is, you respect what he/she does, you respect the contribution he's/she's made. Use the word "respect" every possible time you can. You might even want to get out a thesaurus and look up alternative words for respect so you can say it a hundred ways without overusing the word. But you could use the word "respect" once a day for the next five years and the person would not get tired of hearing how much he/she is respected.

One of the things I've often found in counseling executives and their wives, is that there comes a situation in which the wife or husband has lost respect for the other. In this case, if you have lost respect for someone you care a lot about, and you know he/she needs respect, don't withhold respect—simply define it clearly. Say, "You know, I really respect the way you keep your rose garden." "I really respect the way you keep your house." "I really respect the way you earn a living." "I really respect the way you keep your car." You may not respect his character, you may not respect some aspect of his life, but there is always something you can respect. Whatever it is, be very specific. Don't give blanket respect, but don't withhold respect, because he/she desperately needs respect from you.

If the person you care a lot about needs to be accepted, he/she actually needs to be liked more than he/she needs to be loved, as strange as it may sound to you. How many times have you heard someone say, "I know you *love* me, but do you *like* me?"

This person does not need people to like her/him because of what he/she does for them, not for the mask he/she puts on, nor because he/she is always serving other people. He/she wants to be liked just for who he/she is.

So think of all the ways you can just say to her, "I like you. I like being with you. I like the way you do that. I like the way you wear your hair. I like your choice of clothes. I like watching you. I just like you!"

Focus in the next year on finding which one or two of the eight needs each friend or family member has, and then meet that need. You'll find a very rich and rewarding relational experience with those people. Not only will your needs be met, but you'll meet theirs as well.

## Everyone Is Not Like Me!

One of the most fundamental truths in relating to people that I've ever tried to teach anyone is that "everyone is not like me!"

If you don't need people to be with, don't worry about it. It is perfectly OK to be who you are. Just because your mate needs people a lot doesn't mean you do. If you don't have a lot of friends, it doesn't mean that you are in some way flawed. It may simply mean that you're comfortable being alone. On the other hand, if your mate needs a lot of friends, it doesn't mean he or she is flawed, just different.

Like many people you may be tempted to expect that your mate will be like you, will relate to the kind of people you enjoy relating to, will enjoy having one best friend if you have just one best friend, or can be happy not having a best friend if you don't have a best friend— in short, is just like you, or at least will be when he or she is grown up!

The reality is that you're both grown up already. It's just that you have different relational comfort zones based on childhood experience. Some children relate almost exclusively to the family, and don't have a social life outside the family. If that's how you were, chances are that today you're happy just being with your family and not having a lot of social life. But others were involved in the community, sports, and all kinds of things. Consequently, as adults they feel more comfortable being socially involved. These things are not right or wrong, good or bad. They're simply different. And the sooner you allow your mate to be who he/she is—have the friends he/she wants to have, do what he/

she wants to do—while encouraging her/him to let you have the social patterns you want, the better off you both are.

## A Third Party Helps in Trying to Establish New Communication Patterns with a Spouse or Family

If you are still struggling a little bit with getting your relational needs met and relating to your mate effectively, sometimes a third party really helps. A third party could be a wise friend. Many times I sit down with friends and help them understand their communication patterns. At other times it's a therapist, a mentor, or a pastor. If you find it difficult to communicate these relational needs to your mate, seriously consider the possibility of finding an objective third person you both trust. The other night I sat down with a couple who were having some marital tension, and when we sat down to dinner the husband said, "We've talked a lot about it and you're the one person we both trust." There's nothing wrong with seeking out a person like that.

### Heart Probe:

1. Who are the people you really care about? Make a list. What are their needs? Make a guess. Focus on meeting their needs and see how much it improves your relationship with them.

2. Which one friend, beyond your mate, do you trust the very most? Who is the wisest person you know? The person whom you most enjoy being with, the person you would go to with a serious personal problem? Why not approach that person to be one of your mentors?

3. Who is the third person that you and your mate both trust the most to settle differences, help you through tough spots, and help you maximize your marriage at all points? If you're single, who is the person that you would go to to sort out what you need and how to get your needs met in appropriate ways?

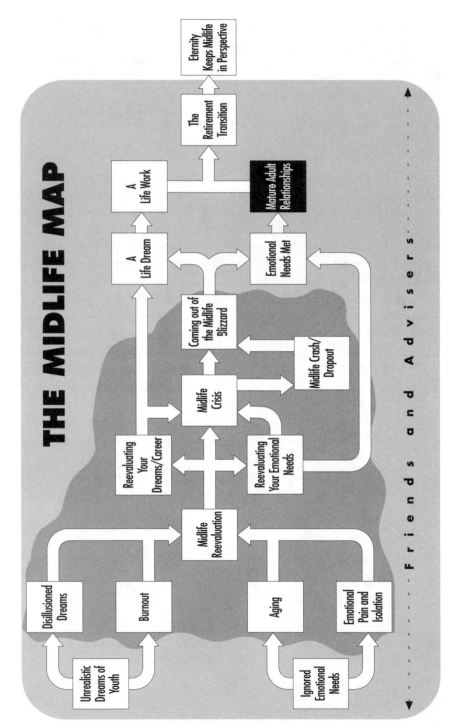

# THE MIDLIFE MAP

Unrealistic Dreams of Youth → Disillusioned Dreams

Burnout

Disillusioned Dreams → Midlife Reevaluation
Burnout → Midlife Reevaluation

Aging → Midlife Reevaluation
Emotional Pain and Isolation → Midlife Reevaluation
Ignored Emotional Needs → Aging
Ignored Emotional Needs → Emotional Pain and Isolation

Midlife Reevaluation → Reevaluating Your Dreams/Career
Midlife Reevaluation → Reevaluating Your Emotional Needs

Reevaluating Your Dreams/Career → Midlife Crisis
Reevaluating Your Emotional Needs → Midlife Crisis

Midlife Crisis → Coming out of the Midlife Blizzard
Midlife Crisis → Midlife Crash/Dropout

Coming out of the Midlife Blizzard → A Life Dream

Midlife Crash/Dropout → Coming out of the Midlife Blizzard

A Life Dream → A Life Work
A Life Dream → Emotional Needs Met

Emotional Needs Met → Mature Adult Relationships

A Life Work → The Retirement Transition
Mature Adult Relationships → The Retirement Transition

The Retirement Transition → Eternity Keeps Midlife in Perspective

- - - Friends and Advisers - - -

© Bobb Biehl 1993

# Map Point 17: Mature Adult Relationships

*When we have our emotional needs met, we are able to maintain healthy, balanced relationships with people over many years.*

About 30 percent of the male executives that I deal with struggle with the issue of manhood. The question is, "Am I really an adult? If I don't know for sure, how can I have adult relationships?" A fairly high percentage of the women I deal with wonder, "Am I an adult? My mother always treats me like a little girl and won't let me grow up."

You feel like an adult when a person of the same sex who you deeply respect, respects you as an equal. I assume you feel very comfortable with your adulthood, and therefore feel comfortable having adult relationships. But if you do not, I would encourage you to discuss this with your mentor. Discuss the adulthood issue, and when your mentor sees you as an adult, it will really help you in the process of affirming your manhood or womanhood.

## Many Levels of Mature Adult Relationships

As you review the names that are on your Christmas card list or on your frequently used phone number list, sort out your adult relationships into different categories. To expect business acquaintances to meet personal needs is an unrealistic expectation. To ask certain people to meet your emotional needs, or for you to invest your personal life in them, would not be productive. But if you can sort out your friends and acquaintances a little bit, it will be much easier both to have your needs met and meet the needs of those who look to you for the same kind of support.

Below you'll find a chart called "My Friends and Acquaintances." This is simply a model, a concept, a construct, a framework . . . you can reproduce it on computer paper so the list can be ten feet long if you like. You can redo the categories using any terms you like. But construct a chart something like this and then start putting names of people on your Friends and Acquaintances Chart.

## MY FRIENDS AND ACQUAINTANCES

| Heart-to-Heart Intimate Friends | Mentors and Confidants | Protégés | Family Members | My Cheerleaders | Social Friends not Personal Friends | Friendly Business Relationships not Friends | Enemies |
|---|---|---|---|---|---|---|---|
| | | | | | | | |

Now let's look at each category a bit more definitively.

### Heart-to-Heart Intimate Friends

These are those rare people in life with whom you are able to drop your guard, take off the mask, drop your defenses. These are your buddies, your pals, your intimate friends. It is rare that an adult will have over a handful of names in this category. You may have only one or two, or possibly not any. Your emotional needs get met primarily by people in this category.

Often we have names out of our past in this category, people who live hundreds of miles from us today. Remember those relationships. You are capable of having intimate relationships today even though you are separated by time, distance, or possibly death from past heart-to-heart intimate friends. Draw on these memories in establishing new relationships. And seriously consider calling, writing, E-mailing friends at a distance and renewing your relationship. Plan a vacation which includes long conversations with such a friend.

One of my very favorite photographs is a picture of my wife, Cheryl, sitting on a balcony, drinking a leisurely, early morning cup of coffee with one of her lifelong friends, Michelle Goebel. There they sit in their housecoats, catching up after a few years and several hundred miles of separation. If I had a caption for the picture, it would be "Heart-to-Heart Friends."

It may interest you to know that probably as many as 50 percent of the men whom I work with do not have a close buddy or friend with whom they could just hang out, pal around, go fishing, golfing, or have fun together. If there isn't a childhood model of having a best friend/buddy, it's very uncomfortable trying to relate to a best friend today. So if you don't have a buddy, you may not feel the need for one. It is not a fatal flaw.

### Mentors and Confidants

Mentors and confidants are people you go to if you have some burden on your heart, need some direction, or want some perspective on life. Who is it you consider your mentor, or your confidant? Who says about you, "You are a person I want to help realize your God-given potential over a lifetime"?

### Protégés

Of which person with less experience than your own do you say to yourself, "This is a person I want to help realize her/his full, God-given potential over a lifetime"?

### Family Members

With which of your family members do you have a genuine relationship, where you occasionally share heart-to-heart? If you had to describe your relationship with each of your relatives, what word would you use for each?

### Cheerleaders

Cheerleaders are the people who energize you. Who are the people in your life that bring you a renewed sense of hope and energy?

### Social Friends

Who are your social friends? The people that you seek out. If you're going out for an evening, if you're going to have a weekend away, or you want to watch a ball game, who is it that you call? Who is it that calls you? They're not necessarily close friends that you have intimate conversations with, but these are people that you like to be with socially. You may only have two or three social friends, or you may have fifty.

### Friendly Business Relationships

These are people you are friendly with professionally, but you wouldn't necessarily socialize with. If you could get a better price somewhere else, you would take it, whereas if you're doing business with a close friend, taking your business somewhere else could be very, very difficult.

### Enemies

Who are your enemies? You may say, "I'm a Christian. I don't have enemies." Why do you think the Bible says "pray for your enemies"? Christians have enemies, just as non-Christians have enemies. If you have enemies, put them in there, because it's important to know who they are. You may not have any. But if you do, put their names right there so that you know with crystal clarity which category they fit in.

If this kind of an exercise is of interest to you, take all the people you know and put their names in one of these categories. This helps you begin to see who takes from you, and who gives to you; who you just enjoy being with, who you go to for counsel. It begins to show you where you've got strength and where you may have a void.

## Couple-to-Couple Relationships

Assuming you're married, you may want to identify those people who both you and your mate feel comfortable with socially. Cheryl and I have found that there are certain couples with whom one of us feels more comfortable or compatible than the other. But there are those special couples with whom *we both feel comfortable* with both husband and wife. So the four of us have a real uniquely compatible chemistry.

You want to identify these "compatible chemistry couples." Be sure to identify those couples, not only in your local community, but anywhere in the world. These may be school friends, friends from growing up years. Keep doing whatever it is that keeps the relationship alive and healthy, even at a distance. A lifelong friendship is too valuable to let it drift into oblivion.

## Memories: Relating As an Adult to Future Generations of the Family

One of the great tragedies is the fact that we die before we are able to relate to our great-great-great-grandchildren—adult to adult. One of my deep regrets was the fact that I knew all four of my grandparents until I was in my late teens and early twenties but did not have the maturity to seek an adult conversation with them about what their lives were like at my age.

One of the things you might want to consider at this point in your life is filling out a memories book. A memories book is simply a guided diary. It tells what your life as an adult has been in the past, what it's like currently, what you hope it will be someday. You write down what you see as an adult, about how you see life, what your experience with God has been, what your experience with people has been, what your experience with your parents has been. It basically helps you write your personal and family history.

There will come a day when your children or grandchildren will want to know what you (dad or mom, aunt or uncle, grandfather or grandma), were like as an adult. What were you thinking? What were your struggles?

It is a way to communicate adult-to-adult with future generations about your experience with God, your struggles, how you came to faith, and actually share your faith with your grandchildren and great-great-great-great-great-grandchildren, ten generations from now. It's an unusual way to look at it, but it's an adult-to-adult conversation/relationship between you and all future generations of your family. Consider it as a possibility.

---

### Heart Probe:

Do you consider yourself an adult? Do you feel like an adult? If not, talk to a mentor and grow in this area as quickly as possible.

What are your most comfortable social patterns? One closest friend, three closest friends, friendly with everyone, close to no one?

Who are the people you enjoy the very most? Who are the people who energize you, the people who make you feel good about life, yourself, the future?

---

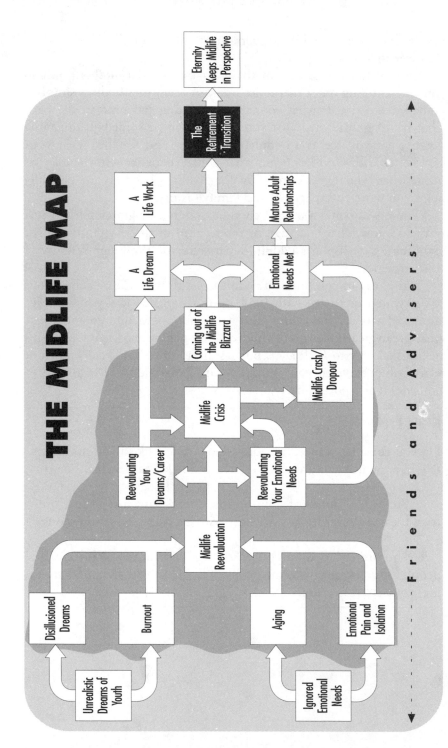

# THE MIDLIFE MAP

**Unrealistic Dreams of Youth** → **Disillusioned Dreams**

**Burnout**

**Disillusioned Dreams** → **Midlife Reevaluation**
**Burnout** → **Midlife Reevaluation**
**Aging** → **Midlife Reevaluation**
**Emotional Pain and Isolation** → **Midlife Reevaluation**

**Ignored Emotional Needs** → **Aging**
**Ignored Emotional Needs** → **Emotional Pain and Isolation**

**Midlife Reevaluation** → **Reevaluating Your Dreams/Career**
**Midlife Reevaluation** → **Reevaluating Your Emotional Needs**

**Reevaluating Your Dreams/Career** → **Midlife Crisis**
**Reevaluating Your Emotional Needs** → **Midlife Crisis**

**Midlife Crisis** → **Coming out of the Midlife Blizzard**
**Midlife Crisis** → **Midlife Crash/Dropout**

**Midlife Crash/Dropout** → **Coming out of the Midlife Blizzard**

**Coming out of the Midlife Blizzard** → **A Life Dream**
**Coming out of the Midlife Blizzard** → **Emotional Needs Met**

**A Life Dream** → **A Life Work**
**Emotional Needs Met** → **Mature Adult Relationships**

**A Life Work** → **The Retirement Transition**
**Mature Adult Relationships** → **The Retirement Transition**

**The Retirement Transition** → **Eternity Keeps Midlife in Perspective**

Friends and Advisers

© Bobb Biehl 1993

# Map Point 18: The Retirement Transition

*Substituting the word "transition" for the traditional word "retirement" offers a whole new perspective on our later years.*

Retirement is a funny word. To some people it's the goal—the point to which all things aim. It's the promise of rest without deadlines, bosses, and responsibilities. To others, retirement is the curse of the century.

The cruel demographic joke is that just as this generation is hitting middle age with unprecedented family responsibilities, corporate America is mustering legions of fifty-somethings out of the work force through early-retirement plans and less compassionate methods. "There is tremendous doubt about the future," says Saveri. "People see their friends getting pink slips. Their M.B.A.s aren't doing them any good now."

Retiring earlier—and living longer—will bring a host of financial, emotional and psychological problems in the years ahead. Today's 50-year-olds still have 20 or 30 more years to live. What are they going to do—and how are they going to pay for it? "The 50s are not the beginning of the end—you have an awful long way to go," says University of Chicago gerontologist Bernice Neugarten, now 76. And that may be the most frightening thought of all.

Professional disappointments weigh especially heavily on men, and they are inevitable even for the most successful. . . . Being forced

out of a job in midlife can be devastating—or liberating, if it brings about a rethinking of what's most important.
(Melinda Beck, "The New Middle Age," *Newsweek*, December 7, 1992, 52–53).

Our perspective on life or any situation plays a very important part in our satisfaction, happiness, and personal fulfillment. The thought of retirement could represent a curse, if the only exposure to retirement was very negative. Unhappy, bored, lonely people—that's retirement according to some. A negative perspective on retirement is the result of the negative examples we have experienced or observed. But there are people who live very satisfying, fulfilling lives in retirement. Find some good models and learn from them. Spend some time with them. Observe how they live. Ask them how they prepared for their retirement years. Change your mind about the retirement years by exposure to positive role models.

For the last ten years I think I've had about three days when I didn't look forward to the day. I look forward to every day, day after day, and enjoy my life immensely. But I would never tire of consulting just because I turn sixty-five. I think the person who dreads retirement is the person who enjoys his work. It really isn't work to him. The person who looks forward to retirement is the person who doesn't look forward to work very much. Either way, at age sixty-five—or whenever it is that you are no longer able to work because of company policy, or physical health, or some other factor—you have to face the prospect of retirement.

I believe we must begin to substitute the word "retirement" with the word "transition." From my perspective, I would like to hear people talk about their age sixty-five "transition," not their age sixty-five "retirement." I would like to have transition parties, not retirement parties. I would like to have people say, "Well, when I transition, here's what I'm going to do."

It's more a matter of shifting gears than it is shutting off the engine. I think the concept of "Planning to Peak in Ten Years" is so very helpful. This concept is described in more detail earlier in chapter 9. I would encourage you, starting five to ten years prior to the time you plan to retire, to develop a "transition" strategy that includes what you will start doing the day you stop working where you work. Begin defining your future steps now.

Let's say, for example, you decide you are going to be an artist when you have more optional time. Start taking art classes five or ten years before you actually retire. By the time you retire you'll have the knowledge and experience to really enjoy your art. You will have what my son, J. Ira, calls, "a refined skill." It's something you've been working at and have in place and ready to go. It's not something you're just getting into. It's something that will fill a lot of hours with very productive work.

Plan to be active in your retirement years. Develop interests that will keep your mind stimulated. Develop physical exercise habits you can continue into your later years. Develop relationships now that will be "lifelong" friends. There is great comfort in knowing that you have friends with whom you can "grow old together."

Many people are finding opportunities to volunteer their time in productive activity. Some have volunteered to work with the Forest Service as campground hosts. They receive a modest income and a trailer space at no charge for the summer—in very beautiful locations. Others have volunteered to observe wildlife, counting their sightings or locations. Others work in hospitals providing information and counsel for families of patients. The list of possibilities is limitless.

Consider spending time being a mentor in your retirement years. Work with people with less experience than you, who look up to you. Have coffee with your young protégés. Help them know how to mature. Help them know how to grow and reach their full potential over their lifetime and yours. Nothing is quite so satisfying as investing your life in another and seeing your life and values extended beyond yourself.

---

## Heart Probe:

What do you look forward to the very most after your age sixty-five "transition"?

What can you do today to start preparing for that activity?

---

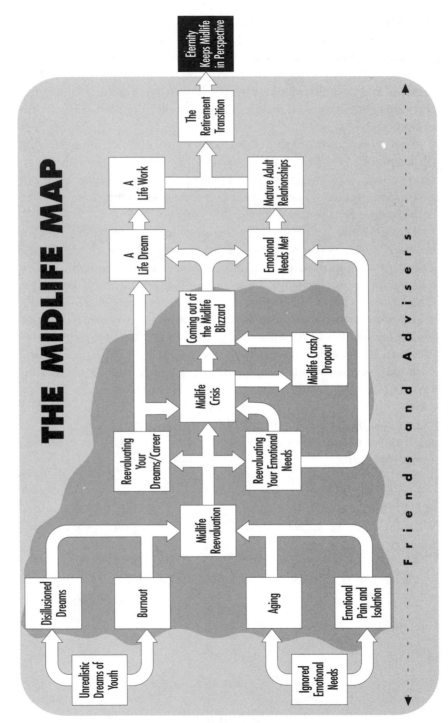

# THE MIDLIFE MAP

Eternity Keeps Midlife in Perspective

The Retirement Transition

A Life Work

A Life Dream

Coming out of the Midlife Blizzard

Midlife Crisis

Midlife Crash/ Dropout

Reevaluating Your Dreams/Career

Reevaluating Your Emotional Needs

Mature Adult Relationships

Emotional Needs Met

Midlife Reevaluation

Disillusioned Dreams

Burnout

Aging

Emotional Pain and Isolation

Unrealistic Dreams of Youth

Ignored Emotional Needs

- - - - Friends and Advisers - - - -

© Bobb Biehl 1993

# Map Point 19: Eternity Keeps Midlife in Perspective

*Our lives will know an end someday in time. Living our lives now with a sense of eternity brings a helpful perspective and hope in dealing with midlife issues.*

There are three words that boggle my mind when I really try to grasp them. The words are eternity, forever, and endless. As hard as my human brain tries to stretch, in about three seconds it goes into overload. Compound the challenge of grasping the *concept* of eternity with the challenge of grasping its *reality!*

When one comes to some clarity in their perspective on life in the context of eternity, all things look quite different.

Today is not all there is. There is eternity. This life will one day come to an end. This thought alone has sobered my judgment on many occasions. The midlife process is probably no more than ten years long, if that. Eternity puts midlife in proper context—a context in which I can live all of life. Even though it doesn't feel like it, I realize that time is passing and that eternity is a reality. Someday I will meet my Maker in the context of eternity and account for how I've lived this life.

## My Single Most Helpful Question in Midlife

By far and away, the most helpful exercise in my midlife years was to wrestle with the single question, "If I could only accomplish three things before I die, what three measurable things would I want to accomplish?" This question made two very profitable contributions to my thinking. First, it focused my thinking on the future and not my current pain. Second, it clarified my highest values in this life. That was a huge help!

The day I defined those three things, my life became clear. It was in one sense like the cable from a tow truck in Map Point 19 attached to my belt dragging me out of the blizzard and pulling me into the next thirty years. And it put me on the right track for what I wanted to accomplish with an eternal perspective in mind.

I don't know how better to tell you how pivotal it was to my life personally—in the middle of this midlife blizzard, this midlife reevaluation—to have a target established thirty or forty years into the future. I would encourage you to ask yourself, "If I could only get three measurable things done sometime before I die and enter eternity, what three measurable things would I want to get done?" You will find that wherever you are in life today, your answer will be extremely focused for you.

## Keeping Eternity As a Part of Your Thinking Is Not Easy in Midlife

The midlife blizzard you've just gone through, from Points 4 through 13, has been happening through time and toward eternity. When you're in the middle of the blizzard, it is extraordinarily difficult to see or care that time and eternity are equally real. But as I began coming out of the midlife blizzard, some of the truths I had understood much earlier in life began to come back to me. When I was maybe 22 years old I came to the conclusion that, "Life is to be lived with a death perspective." We should live all of our life as we would like to have lived it when we lie on our deathbed at 117 years of age. Looking back over your life, you will not want to say, "I wish I'd lived life this way." Or, "If I'd only done this or that." Living life with minimal regrets is a worthy value. As you reflect on your life at this time, decide what is important to you in the context of eternity.

Today, if we were to sit down at your very favorite coffee shop in the world, and you were to ask me, "Bobb, of all the thoughts about God and eternity—bottom line, which actually helped you the very most in the process of coming out of your midlife years?" There are three focusing thoughts, which have been disproportionately helpful to me personally in gaining perspective on life. We have:

ONE short life (even if we live to be 100 years old) to live, in light of eternity.

ONE eternal destination: heaven or hell.

ONE way to get to heaven. Jesus said, "I am the way, the truth, and the life, No man comes to the Father but by Me."

Your mind and heart may be in a completely different place than mine when I came out of my midlife years. But, these thoughts about God and eternity really helped focus my thinking in those early days. These three truths keep shaping my day-to-day decisions as I reflect on the nanosecond that I draw my last breath on this earth, leave time as we know it, and enter eternity.

---

## Heart Probe:

If you could only accomplish three things sometime before you die, what three measurable things would you want to accomplish?

How do you view God today?

What do you actually believe about Him today? (Not what other people say you should believe, not what other people think you believe)

What do you actually believe about your eternal destiny today?

---

# Appendix A: Emotional Balance Chart

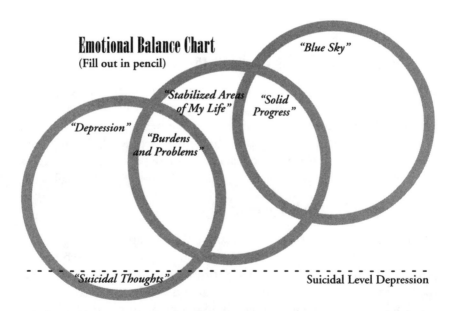

**Emotional Balance Chart**
(Fill out in pencil)

"Blue Sky"

"Stabilized Areas of My Life"

"Solid Progress"

"Depression"

"Burdens and Problems"

"Suicidal Thoughts"

Suicidal Level Depression

Whenever I feel like I'm riding too high and can't seem to come down to earth, I get out the *Emotional Balance Chart* and look at my negative realities. At the same time, when I feel depressed and everything is "falling apart," I get out the *Emotional Balance Chart* and

t the positive realities. It is one of the ways I have
d to stay "in the middle of reality." (Incidentally, both
eed constant updating. That's why we suggest that the
*ance Chart* be kept in pencil.)

## Put a High Bottom on Your Bottom

Whenever you get to the depression stage, develop a series of action steps and Scriptures which can keep you from going into suicidal thinking. For example:
1. Do something for someone else, sing, praise God, count your blessings, take a walk, exercise, do something meaningful, talk to a friend, see others who are less fortunate, volunteer for some activity, admit that the worst that could happen is not fatal, check your diet.
2. Some Scriptures for coping include: Romans 8:28; Luke 16:19-31; Philippians 4:8; Psalm 27:15; Philippians 4:19; Hebrews 12:14; Proverbs 3:5-6; Psalm 37:1; Psalm 103:10-12; Philippians 4:13; James 1:2-8; Psalm 27:1.

## Study Your Process of Going Up and Down

Depression comes in stages. Study how you begin to get depressed and what the next step is and the next. Soon you begin to learn your own patterns. When you start the descent, you can begin looking at positive realities, and it helps you keep from becoming depressed. Talking with a close friend can also help you stay out of depression. Talk with a friend about how to work your way out of negative reality areas.

## Carry a List of Positive Realities with You

Make an exhaustive list of all the positive things happening in your life which are real and proven. Whenever you begin to get discouraged, pull out the list and review it many times to see that "all is not lost," the "bottom has not fallen out," and that you will in fact "make it."

The *Emotional Balance Chart* is like a parachute out of blue sky and a lifesaver on the sea of self-pity and despair. Whenever you start getting too high or too low, get out your *Emotional Balance Chart* and work your way back toward the middle using the above process.

The *Emotional Balance Chart* is a confidential tool for you to use. But if you should choose to share it with someone close to you, it can

166

be a very helpful process to let them see your emotional patterns.

At very best, life is a struggle for balance. It is my prayer that by using the *Emotional Balance Chart* you will be able to maintain your sense of personal balance.

If you find yourself "stuck" in a depression, consult your doctor or counselor for specific help.

# Explanation of Terms

1. *Blue Sky* (unrealistically positive)

   Definition: Any idea, thought, plan, program, or dream which is unproven at present—no matter how much potential.

   Examples:
   - Someday we'll make millions!
   - Next year at this time we will be flying high!
   - Can you imagine the potential?
   - This is a "sure winner"
   - I'm "sure" this will work—soon!

2. *Solid Progress* (positive reality)

   Definition: Very positive milestones

   Examples:
   - Track record
   - Results/achievements
   - Accomplishments
   - Records set
   - Money in the bank
   - Completed projects/progress
   - Happy family
   - Health

3. *Stabilized* (objective reality)

   Definition: Those things which simply exist. Neither extreme positive nor extreme negative—they just are! But they are important pieces.

   Examples:
   - Bills are paid—no extra in the bank

- Have a car—not new or old
- Have a job—not ideal or unemployed

4. *Burdens/Problems* (negative reality)

   Definition: Heavy negative realities—not imaginary but needing to be lived or dealt with in reality.

   Examples:
   - Terminal illness
   - A major physical handicap
   - Major indebtedness
   - Divorce
   - Credit overextension
   - House desperately needs paint
   - Severely overweight

5. *Depression* (negative unrealistic)

   Definition: Negative thoughts which have no basis in reality.

   Examples:
   - Worries
   - Phobias
   - "Blue Funk"
   - "The Dumps"

6. *Suicidal Thoughts* (total, acute self-centeredness—negative)

   Definition: So negative life doesn't seem worth living.

   Examples:
   - At the bottom—thoughts of suicide
   - Suicide attempts

\* The Emotional Balance Chart is used by written permission from Masterplanning Group International.

# Appendix B: Golden Handcuffs

## Introduction to Golden Handcuffs

BEFORE plunging from an established position in business into "the Lord's work . . . as a full-time Christian worker" there are a few tough questions which need to be answered. If you are considering such a move, or have someone you are about to hire who is . . . this is must reading—as soon as possible. The article does not discourage this type of transition . . . but helps you "Count the Cost."

### EIGHT QUESTIONS TO ASK YOURSELF BEFORE YOU BREAK THE "GOLDEN HANDCUFFS"

"I'm not sure I can leave the 'Golden Handcuffs' to join a Christian organization . . . my company has me locked in with money and benefits." This very candid confession came from a close friend who was making $150,000 salary, plus all benefits.

Was this a "lack of faith statement" or a simple realistic evaluation of life in the upper strata of Corporate America?

Before you take the plunge and jump headlong from business or industry into a Christian organization, may I suggest that you consider the following questions very carefully.

1.  **Have You Carefully Considered the Implications of the Changed Focus (Slightly Overstated) from *Profit to People*?**

    A business exists primarily to make a profit.

    A ministry exists primarily to meet the needs of people . . . which is often not profitable, but actually takes money.

    This is an extremely hard transition to make in many cases. This difference has implications in the amount of time spent on various projects, the style in which you lead, and the money you do or don't make.

2.  **Have You Carefully Considered the Real Difference in *People Perspective*?**

    Many people make the mistaken assumption that the difference between a Christian and non-Christian organization is that one is legally a profit corporation and the other a not-for-profit organization. Or, that one calls itself Christian while the other does not.

    May I suggest that the real difference, where the "rubber meets the road," is your perspective of people as a means or an end.

    The organization or corporation which views people as valuable individuals to be developed for their own benefit in the process of reaching a goal or completing a task is functioning on a Christian premise. The organization which assumes people to be a means to accomplish a project is in serious danger of non-Christian exploitation of people even though it may be a church or Christian organization.

    But, the question before you today is this, "In your heart of hearts, have you seen people in the past as disposable tools to be used and discarded like a broken wrench or an obsolete computer?" If so, you may not find yourself at all comfortable working in a Christian organization. On the other hand, because of your truly Christian perspective on people, you may find it much more comfortable in a Christian setting than where you work today.

3. **Are You Ready for the *Trauma of Transition* Which Comes Whenever You Change Career Directions?**

If you are a salesman and become an accountant or vice versa, there will be a major 1–3 year transition. Your self-image, your sense of competence and confidence, your identity, your salary, and many more dimensions will experience traumatic change even if you stay within the *same* company.

But, to make a change from a business or industrial position where you have a major position, status, and expertise to an area where you are in some ways "starting over" will be a 1–5 year adjustment not only for you but your family as well.

4. **Are You Psychologically Ready for the *Difference in Size* Between the Company You Work for Today and the Christian Organization You Are Considering?**

On many occasions you may have heard people compare "business" and the ministry saying, "Business does things this way and that way." A more accurate statement may be *"Big Business* does it this or that way."

What is the budget difference between the organization you are now with and the one you are considering?

| | Present Company | Considering |
|---|---|---|
| Your Salary & Benefits | $_____ | $_____ |
| Your Support Budget (secretaries, office equipment, supplies, cont. educ., budget, etc.) | $_____ | $_____ |
| Travel Budget | $_____ | $_____ |
| Total Organizational | $_____ | $_____ |

Remember, the operational style and approach of a Big Business and a small business are drastically different. But the difference between the style of a Big Business and a small ministry (under 3 million) can be devastating. Be prepared for this transition . . . it is tough!

5. **Is Your Family Ready for the** *Salary Transition?*

Many people know up-front that a Christian organization, which doesn't seek to make a profit, couldn't be expected to have the money available for salaries which a major profit company has.

But, when it comes to a $23,000–$50,000 salary cut to "serve the Lord" the practical realities need to be kept very clearly in mind.

It is critical to sit down with the family and think and pray through such a reduction. Don't be surprised . . . and disillusioned . . . in a year or two because you didn't calculate the cost properly today.

6. **Are You Ready for the Differences in** *Organizational Phase* **That the Change You Are Considering Represents?**

Every organization goes through three basic phases:

Design—where everything is being "designed the first time."
Development—where the ideas are being developed and where there are only a few stated policies or procedures.
Administrative—where most programs and procedures are fairly routine.

If you enjoy the administrative phase and the organization you are considering is in the development phase or vice versa, this change can be extremely threatening or stifling.

Any brand-new program represents a time of risks, traumatic transition, and evolution for a period of three years to "get off the ground." If you need a stable organized environment, with a substantial budget to feel settled, this first three years can be extremely painful.

7. **Are You Ready for a Major Shift in the Business** *Background* **of Your "Boss"?**

In business or industry your manager or vice president may have a M.B.A. from Harvard . . . but not one day of seminary. Your new senior pastor or executive director may have a Ph.D. from seminary but not a single course in business.

Have your eyes wide open to the implications of this difference and don't expect too much of your "Boss" or make too harsh a comparison.

8. **Are You Ready for the Differences Between a Staff of Paid Personnel and a Staff of Volunteers?**

A volunteer staff is both exciting (for they eagerly want to help!) and frustrating (for they are sometimes not as well-trained, dependable, or long term).

In conclusion, let me again state clearly that I am *not* saying "stay in business or industry." The only counsel this article is trying to give is that which Jesus gave . . .

> "Before
> You build a house,
> Carefully
> Count the cost . . .
> Lest you leave the house half built and
> The world
> Will look
> And laugh."

# Appendix C: Heart Talk with the Father

Secrets. We all have them. Secret thoughts, feelings, fears, and memories that simply can't be told to anyone. What are the things in your life that you simply cannot tell anyone? But, on the other hand, if you don't, you feel as though you'll explode! These are the things you can tell your Father in heaven.

One thing we need to understand clearly is that feelings have no morality. They are neither right nor wrong. It's how we handle them that makes the difference. It is not wrong to feel anger, nor can we help it on certain occasions, but we can decide not to kill someone. We make the choice of whether or not to deal with our anger in a godly way. Ephesians 4:26 says, "In your anger do not sin."

Sometimes it helps to actually write out things we would like to tell God, because writing is often easier than verbalizing, and can even be a key to understanding our own inner feelings more clearly. When we are unable to express our deepest feelings, we are fortunate that the Holy Spirit understands even our groanings and can interpret them. We don't have to be articulate; we don't even have to put the feelings into words. He knows our hearts.

Until we admit how we really feel in the deepest recesses of our hearts, it's hard to actually deal with our feelings.

## Heart Talk

Heart talk with the Father is simply telling God, in any way you can or care to, what's in the deepest part of your heart—the things you can't tell anyone else! Talking with the Father about what's in your heart can be done while riding in a car, walking in the woods, or strolling along the beach. You can *tell* Him things, *yell* Him things, *scream*, *weep*, even *groan* Him things! He hears it all.

Even though Jesus talked so much about our hearts, it's sometimes difficult to grasp the real meaning of the term "heart" as used in the Scripture. The closest I can come to understanding it is to describe it as that personal part of us that we share with no one.

If our earthly fathers were not approachable, it can be difficult to go to the Heavenly Father and confide in Him. For some, even saying, "Our Father, which art in heaven," triggers a flash of anger because of mistreatment by their earthly fathers. That's a good starting point. Express the profound disappointment you have in your own earthly father. You may begin to resolve some of your anger right there.

## Jesus' Model

When Jesus was on earth, He modeled this open heart talk with the Father. While He was in the desert, He said, "Now My heart is troubled, and what shall I say, 'Father, save Me from this hour'? No, it is for this reason I came to this hour. Father, glorify Your name!" (John 12:27-28) And in the Garden of Gethsemane, as He anticipated His own crucifixion, the Scripture tells us He sweat drops of blood. He expressed His deepest feelings to His Father as He prayed, "Father, if it is possible, may this cup be taken from Me. Yet not as I will, but as You will" (Matt. 26:39). Then on the cross His heart cried out for all to hear, "My God, My God, why have You forsaken Me?" (27:46) Jesus had the ability to express His deepest reality to the Father—sometimes in a groan or a cry, sometimes in a question, sometimes in a statement.

## Ten Questions Which Can Help You with Your Heart Talk to the Father

1. What is the single greatest *disappointment* in your life?

   2. What *family skeleton* do you keep hidden that you would like to share in a heart talk with the Father?

   3. What *broken relationships* have devastated you emotionally?

4. What are your *future hopes*, the things that other friends can't comprehend or believe at this point?

5. What are the *secrets of your soul* that you would like to confess to the Father out loud? (These can be things as simple as a confession of speeding in traffic to a crime as serious as murder, rape, or grand theft.)

6. What *decisions or problems* are you struggling with that are causing you great stress of heart? (They may be decisions or problems you can't even share with your spouse at this stage, or your closest friend.)

7. What are the *feelings* you can't express: fears, anger, feelings about your family, your friends, your work?

8. What *inadequacy, self-doubt, temptation, failures* have you felt in the past that you've never been able to admit to anyone?

9. What *exasperates you, frustrates you, angers you*, takes you to your limit of patience? Ask the Father to give you His perspective on the things that frustrate and anger you.

10. What are the *lingering questions* you've always wanted to ask someone, but there has never been anyone to ask?

## Fresh Perspective

Heart talk with the Father frequently gives us new perspective options. It's like talking with a friend who remains silent, but when we're finished with our conversation, we say, "It really helps just to talk about it."

Frequently the Father talks to us in one of two ways. Dr. Bill Bright, founder and president of Campus Crusade for Christ, describes them as "illumination, where things just begin to make sense to us; and instruction, where God actually talks to us and gives us certain perspectives."

Even if we do not gain a fresh perspective or a new option on something we're dealing with, the one thing heart talk with the Father does promise to do is help us gain an eternal perspective on our problem or situation. Simply by turning to God we are moving from the temporal limitations of time to a perspective that's enlarged by eternity. That's a major perspective change on any problem, situation, or feeling.

## Appropriate Pressure Release

When we're feeling great pressure, frustration, anger, or disappointment, one tendency is to explode, blow up, or break confidences because of the sheer pressure we feel. Taking our feelings to the Father frees us to move on and resolve some of the anger—sometimes without even needing to discuss it with another human being.

## The Holy Spirit's Role

Scripture describes the Holy Spirit as a comforter, healer, and listener. He never tires of listening, is always awake, understands with a perfect understanding our human frailties, takes all of what we say and interprets it properly to the Father in heaven.

Loneliness of the soul is the deepest kind of loneliness that exists on the face of the earth. It cannot be shared with another human being. But you don't have to experience loneliness of heart if you'll choose to experience a heart-to-heart talk with the Father!

"In the same way the Spirit helps us in our weakness. We do not know what we ought to pray for, but the Spirit Himself intercedes for us with groans that words cannot express, and He who searches our hearts knows the mind of the Spirit, because the Spirit intercedes for the saints in accordance with God's will." Romans 8:26-27

"Peace I leave you. My peace I give you. I do not give as the world gives. Do not let your hearts be troubled. Do not be afraid." John 14:27

Heart Talk with the Father . . . an article which appeared in the Briargate Media News/Published by Focus on the Family . . . May 1995 edition.

# Appendix D: Presidential Profile

*A framework for defining your strengths and growth areas so you can be ready as your dreams become reality!*

## Introduction

The Presidential Profile has several applications including:

1. Evaluating a current President to see what's missing or where growth areas are recommended.
2. Analyzing a candidate for a Presidential position to determine his or her areas of strength and needed growth.
3. Helping a person who wants to someday be a President identify the areas in which he needs to grow, so he will be ready when opportunity knocks.

This checklist has been developed from over 21,000 hours of interaction with Presidents throughout a seventeen-year period, but is not to be counted on as 100 percent complete. If it can give you 80 to 95 percent of what you're looking for in spotting strengths, problems, or defining growth areas, its mission will have been accomplished.

As you go through this profile, rate yourself or your current candidate by each attribute on a scale of 1–10 with 10 being a great strength and 1 being a major weakness.

(**A note on gender:** This resource has been written using almost exclusively "he, him, or his," rather than "she or her." This is for ease of reading only, and is not intended to be exclusive. "He," in this resource, can be read "the person," "the candidate," or "me," as applicable.)

*A President is:*

1. Action Focused
2. Big-picture Focused
3. Charismatic (Personality and Style)
4. Confident
5. Communicative
6. Decisive
7. Financially Astute (Organizationally)
8. Financially Successful (Personally)
9. Focused
10. Healthy and Energetic
11. Inspiring
12. Integrated
13. Natural at Leading
14. Market Sensitive
15. Networked
16. Organizationally Matched
17. Positive in Attitude (Genuine/Consistent)
18. Presidential in Bearing, Class, and Style
19. Relational (with Male and Female)
20. Respected
21. Smart
22. Socially Skilled
23. Spiritually Mature
24. Spouse Supported
25. Successful (Personally)
26. Teachable
27. Team-building (Committed)
28. Trustworthy
29. Visionary
30. "Win Big" Focused vs. "Get By" Focused

### 1. Action Focused

A great President has to *do*, to take action, to move, to make things happen. He cannot just sit around thinking and/or talking. He needs uncommon *courage* to take necessary actions in anxious and stressful situations.

*Effectiveness* (finding *right* solutions) must be the focus, not efficiency (finding *quick* solutions), because all the action in the world in the wrong direction can amount to very little.

• As an ACTION FOCUSED person I would rate myself _____.

### 2. Big-picture Focused

A President must have a basic understanding of the key components in a *healthy organization*, and how they work together to create health and strength within the working environment.

A President needs to be *systems based* and understand the value of creating systems to produce long-term results, not just single time activities or projects. Without systems in place an organization cannot, and will not, grow.

Once the big picture is clear, the President needs to have a *strategic focus* concentrating on the very few critical moves that will make the most difference. He must avoid getting absorbed in the routine detail of running the organization.

- As a BIG-PICTURE FOCUSED PERSON I would rate myself _____.

### 3. Charismatic (Personality and Style)

A President needs to have *showmanship without showing off.* Things need to be done in a way that is above average, unique, special, memorable, classy, and slightly better than the person experiencing it would have thought to do it.

The President needs to be a *"pied piper" of people*—a person people enjoy following because of his charisma, charm, and personal magnetism. The people who follow should be strong men and women, not a collection of people who are simply dependent on the leader for affirmation and self-confidence.

The person needs *a winning smile, a sense of humor, and a charming personality.* Ideally, a President will present himself well physically. He should be attractive, but he need not look like a high fashion model.

- As a CHARISMATIC (IN PERSONALITY AND STYLE) person I would rate myself _____.

### 4. Confident

There must be a proper *balance between drive* (toward goals and dreams of the future) and *being driven* (from haunts and phobic fears of the past). Ideally, the President has a sense of destiny and has resolved any sense of debilitating phobic fears because of childhood.

The person needs to be *an authority* on some subject resulting in a genuine sense of life confidence. A sense of true authority or mastery in any area of life can help a person have a sense of generalized confidence in all areas of life.

This life confidence must be communicated *without arrogance or pride.* It must be genuine confidence, not a mask of confidence.

- As a CONFIDENT person I would rate myself _____.

### 5. Communicative

A President needs to be a person who *speaks* in an inspiring way. The speech style may be dynamic or quiet, but either way it's inspiring. It is critical to have the ability to move people emotionally from where they are to where the executive would like them to be.

A President needs to have a good *media presence*. In today's society it is ideal to have a person who is a strong communicator, not only in person, but also through radio, television, and written communication.

The President must be a *salesperson*. He must be able to sell "snowballs to Eskimos," as the old saying goes. It is vital to have this communication skill, whenever required, to close the deal, to cause the crowd to march, or to recruit the person he wants on the team.

• As a COMMUNICATIONS STRONG person I would rate myself _____.


### 6. Decisive

This person needs a *history of wise decisions*, decisions he made which turned out to be right.

A President needs an ability to *analyze, synthesize*, and *decide quickly* and *accurately*. He must have a good *sense of timing* about when he has analyzed and synthesized enough, what the right decision is, and when it is time to act!

A sense of *decision-making confidence* is required, once the decision has been made. Unless significant new information requires a fresh evaluation, there should not be a double-mindedness that keeps him revisiting or rethinking critical decisions.

• As a DECISIVE person I would rate myself _____.


### 7. Financially Astute (Organizationally)

A great President has the *ability to generate income* in order to generate working capital! This is a bottom line, nonnegotiable, critical consideration for any President.

He also has to have the ability to personally or managerially develop systems to *control expenses*. Part of controlling expenses is being good at *negotiating agreements*.

He has to be wise in *managing and maximizing any reserves available*. Knowing where to put extra capital is critical wisdom for a

President, as is knowing how to *spend wisely!* Foolish spending can cost an organization its cash reserve very quickly.

A President cannot be *penny wise and pound foolish.* Many people lose the big picture when it comes to money and think, "How can we get by?" rather than, "How can we win big?"

- As a FINANCIALLY ASTUTE person I would rate myself
_____.

### 8. Financially Successful (Personally)

A President needs to be *personally secure financially*—making his house payments regularly, not facing bankruptcy, and not worried about excessive debt. If he can't manage his own home well, he will likely find it extremely difficult to manage the finances of an organization.

Without personal success, it may be difficult for him to entertain well, to be confident among financially successful peers, or to present a successful image on behalf of the organization.

When you are in his home, riding in his car, or seeing him in a social setting apart from the office, you need to have a sense that he is a successful person.

This person needs to have a *history of having or getting capital.* Wherever he has gone, or whatever he has done, he has a history of financial success, not just the potential for it.

- As a FINANCIALLY SUCCESSFUL person I would rate myself
_____.

### 9. Focused

A great President needs to have a *dream* of what life will be like someday. Ideally, the question of *Lifework* has been settled and this organization is where he plans to spend the rest of his professional life.

Once the big picture is settled, you need a person who *thinks one to two years in the future* and has his *top ten goals/problems defined* for the coming year.

Once the year's plan is in place you need someone who thinks in terms of *intense quarters* asking Steve Douglass' question, "What are the three things we can do in the next ninety days to make a 50 percent difference?"

- As a FOCUSED person I would rate myself_____.

### 10. Healthy and Energetic

A President needs to be *naturally enthusiastic*, to have a sense of energy, drive, and excitement about the future. Of course, this is communicated in different ways according to personal style. Some people whisper when they get excited, some people scream.

One of the things that is often overlooked in choosing a President is the question, "Is he *travel durable?*" How many days can he go without resting? How long can he travel? How many short nights and long days with intense meetings can he endure?

The person has to have either *high energy or deep stamina*, one or the other is required to be an effective President.

• As a HEALTHY AND ENERGETIC person I would rate myself _____.

### 11. Inspiring

The first way to inspire people is to be a *model* of what you're trying to get them to do or be. Unless this person can model, at a fundamental level, what he is asking his team to do, it will be difficult for him to motivate the team in that direction.

A great leader has to have the ability to *appeal to the noble*, grand, majestic, and heroic on his team, especially when coming up against enemies like time, competition, discouragement, and man's ultimate enemy, Satan.

He needs to inspire people without resorting to fear, threats, or other kinds of negative manipulation. Ideally, the motivation is positive and intrinsic (inside the head) rather than extrinsic (relying on "carrot and stick"). Many great leaders work with "carrot and stick" motivation. This is less than ideal and is short-lived when compared with intrinsic motivation. Intrinsic motivation implants dreams in the hearts of men and women and gives them a vehicle to accomplish their dreams.

• As an INSPIRATIONAL person I would rate myself _____.

### 12. Integrated

A President representing an organization needs a deep sense of *integrity* (what you see is what you get). If you have an executive with "masks" where he is one thing in public, and very, very different in private, you have got a lack of integrity. That eventually spells trouble with a capital "T."

Another aspect of integration is being a fully *integrated adult*. The person should be comfortable with:

His sense of authority/specialty.

His manhood (her womanhood).

His identity. He should know that he is okay without having to be more like someone else.

There also needs to be an *integration between theory and practice*. A lot of Presidents have all their theory right but their practice doesn't back it up.

Finally, there needs to be a sense of *stable balance* among the seven areas of life.

(1) Family/marriage
(2) Financial
(3) Personal growth
(4) Physical
(5) Professional
(6) Social
(7) Spiritual

The person needs to have the ability to correct a severe imbalance quickly.

- As an INTEGRATED person I would rate myself _____.


### 13. Natural at Leading

There are many kinds of leaders, but all have in common the ability to answer the questions, "*What do we do next?*" "*Why is that important?*" "*How do we bring the appropriate resources to bear on the need at hand?*"

A leader has been defined as someone with people following him. One aspect of being a good President is that *strong men and strong women naturally want to follow* him and would likely follow him even if they were not paid to do so.

A strong President simply assumes that people will want to follow him. He enjoys leading, enjoys setting the agenda, and assumes that people will want to be a part of it. He enjoys *leading naturally*.

- As a person who LEADS NATURALLY I would rate myself _____.

### 14. Market Sensitive

A wise President is *market sensitive*. He is acutely aware of what his followers think, feel, need, want, believe, and fear. He also has the ability to adapt the presentation of his cause, mission, or project in light of where the market is.

A wise President has to be bottom line *profit focused* when it comes to the marketing program. It isn't enough to have pretty ads or be creating a nice image. He has to know whether the advertising paid for itself or not. Did it make money? What are its rollout potentials in terms of funding our future dreams?

A wise President has a *nose for the big winners*. He has a sense of what will win, and what will win big. He picks winners and rolls them out, *seizing the moment* in the marketing strategy.

- As MARKET SENSITIVE I would rate myself _____.

### 15. Networked

The first network a great President needs to turn to is his *own team*— people who are available, willing, and eager to help.

The *next network* a leader needs is within their *own market*, within their *own general interest* areas. For example: ministers, coaches, single parents, buyers, sellers—they need to have a network established in their market. A person who tries to be a "Lone Ranger" will not have the rich resources and wealth of ideas of someone who is backed up by a trusted network of advisers and peers.

The President needs to have the appropriately developed network *locally*, *nationally*, and, in fact, *internationally*, as required.

- As NETWORKED I would rate myself _____.

### 16. Organizationally Matched

It is very important that the *social aspects*, personally and organizationally, are matched. A tennis-playing pastor does not fit in a bowling church or vice-versa.

The next match is *size*. There are many people who like being a "big fish in a small pond" and many others who like being a "small fish in a big pond." Not only is it a matter of liking but a matter of doing well. Is this the right-size organization for this person to lead?

*Dream compatibility* is a third organizational match. Are the

President's dreams in a consistent, congruent direction with the dreams, goals, and direction of the organization? Often there are a few degrees difference in the dream direction, and it creates continuous stress on the individual, as well as the organization.

- As ORGANIZATIONALLY MATCHED I would rate myself _____.

### 17. Positive in Attitude (Genuine/Consistent)

A strong leader needs to have a positive attitude—a *can do* attitude!—especially against major odds. His team needs to believe that if they're two touchdowns behind in the last two minutes of the game, "they can still win this thing." This requires a sense of almost *indomitable optimism* with a *dash of realism.*

A President needs to have a *positive perception of his people*, their spouses, and their families. This person really likes, and is excited about, his own spouse, family, team, and people in general.

He needs to have a *positive excitement about the future.* The President that is discouraged and dull concerning the future is not going to lead a team in a positive, inspiring manner.

- As POSITIVE IN ATTITUDE I would rate myself _____.

### 18. Presidential in Bearing, Class, and Style

The President needs *presidential style—personally.* When you meet him, you sense that he is a world-class leader, a top person, a person who is on the "A" team—just by his appearance, image, and bearing.

When you visit a President's home, you ought to get an impression of *presidential-level class.* The person applying for a position who has not had a presidential position or income may not have a large home or expensive car, but everything he has in his home makes it obvious that if he had more money, ability, or position, he could handle it.

Ideally, you want to get a feeling of the *organizational setting* in which he works. Does he have a sense of presidential class in terms of standards of excellence in the office setting? Ask yourself, "If he took over our organization, and our image became what his current organizational image is, would we be excited or disappointed?"

- As PRESIDENTIAL IN BEARING AND CLASS I would rate myself _____.

### 19. Relational (With Male and Female)

A President has to *love people*. He doesn't have to be overly expressive of that love, but his team and the people around him must have an awareness that their President really cares for and loves people.

The great President needs to be a "*heart reader*." He needs to be able to see their dreams, their motives, their fears, their aspirations, and what makes them tick, in order to get a reading on what has been heretofore "hidden in their hearts."

Along with that sensitivity, a top leader must be willing to challenge and confront his team members. Three words that give perspective in confrontation are care, honesty, and fairness. (e.g., I *care* too much about you not to be *honest* with you, and in *fairness* to the whole team I must tell you . . . )

The leader's sense of fairness results in his being the protector and champion of his team.

- As a RELATIONAL person I would rate myself _____.

### 20. Respected

Without team and constituent *respect*, a leader is in very deep weeds.

First of all, a leader must be a person of *character*. He has to be a genuine person with integrity, honesty, faithfulness, trustworthiness—all of the moral virtues that make a person strong against even the "stiff winds of life."

Second, the President must have an *impeccable reputation*. If one were to ask 100 people, "What is this person's reputation?" the responses would all be overwhelmingly positive. *Reputation in our society has almost become as important as reality.* It should never be thus, but reputation is a critical dimension for the President of any organization.

Third, he needs to have a reputation of being *a well-known leader in his field*. Having such a reputation requires visibility, credibility, and ability that is recognized and respected by his colleagues.

- As RESPECTED I would rate myself _____.

### 21. Smart

Being a President of any organization requires a wide range of variables to be kept in focus and balanced at any one time. Thus, a high intelligence is required—not academic intelligence as much as personal brightness.

One aspect of personal brightness is having *strategic instincts.* By this, I mean the ability to get a feel for a situation and have a (conscious or unconscious) process to define almost instantly the critical moves required, taking into account the entire contextual reality and the direction in which the team needs to move.

A great leader has the ability to take the incredible complexity of an organization, project, or situation, and come to a profoundly simple understanding of it. As a result, he arrives at a profoundly simple directional decision. He avoids being confused by the complexity. He avoids misfiring in a lot of directions. But, he has one to three very critical moves to lead in the direction the team needs to go.

- As SMART I would rate myself _____.

### 22. Socially Skilled

The first and foremost dimension of social skills is a *class match.* As was mentioned earlier, a tennis playing pastor will not be comfortable at a bowling church, and a bowling pastor will not be comfortable at a tennis playing church. This sometimes unfortunate rule of thumb holds true, no matter what the organization.

The President *must be comfortable at all levels of the society with which he will need to work.* It is critical that a President be comfortable at a country club and equally happy in a cornfield, if that is required by the organization's constituency.

Ideally, the President of an organization is *extremely comfortable leading the "A team" socially.* The President is one who has the ability to relate to, play with, and feel comfortable leading really strong people in a social setting as well as an organizational one. This is a critical dimension of choosing a President.

- As SOCIALLY SKILLED I would rate myself _____.

### 23. Spiritually Mature

Great Presidents need to be *spiritual examples.* This does not mean they have to subscribe to every trifle of some denomination's complete list of doctrinal positions—unless you are hiring a spiritual teacher. However, adherence to at least the essential doctrines of the historical Christian church may be appropriate for many positions, especially in Christian organizations.

Great Presidents need maturity which allows for spiritual flexibility and the accommodation of gray areas, not just a black and white "Religious Rigidity." The gray areas (those areas which are not directly addressed in Scripture) must be recognized and dealt with in a flexible, realistic, and ethical way.

The other dimension of spiritual maturity for the executive is that there must be a *trustworthy integration* between spiritual "talk" and what the team senses (by observing the "walk") is genuinely in the person's heart. Hypocrisy is easy to detect and can easily destroy credibility in leadership.

• As SPIRITUALLY MATURE I would rate myself _____.

### 24. Spouse Supported

The President's *spouse must be an asset* in every dimension from image to attitude.

The *role* of the spouse must be clearly defined, accepted, and comfortable to the spouse for the President to feel content, confident, and happy in his environment.

The spouse must be *positively excited*, not only about the role the President is playing, but also about the role he or she has in making the entire organization what it is capable of becoming.

In today's world, many wives are uncomfortable with and reject the "traditional role" of the wife. The role the spouse plays in a church or organization can vary widely depending on personal interests. But whatever the role is chosen to be, *there must be positive excitement for the President's position* in the organization, approval of the organization itself, and satisfaction with the spouse's opportunity to serve.

If the President has no spouse, he should be a *confident and content single*. He has the responsibility to live uprightly in his situation. He must present himself as committed to his work, his church, his organization, and his peers with no indication or cause for suspicion of promiscuity.

• As SPOUSE SUPPORTED I would rate myself _____.

190

### 25. Successful (Personally)

The President needs *a long history of goals reached or problems solved.* As you look back over his history, there needs to be a wide variety of things done right, conclusions reached, and results achieved. In short, there is evidence that he has been successful.

There needs to be a sense in which this person, starting early in his career, has been promoted frequently, *gone "up the ladder,"* and landed at or near the top in a wide variety of settings—or, at least landed near the top in one or two.

The wise choice for a President may also include one who has *failed and come back.* The person needs to have had an experience in which something he did has not worked the way he hoped. In essence, it has *"failed."* But he has managed a *high integrity comeback* where he did not simply avoid the issues, lie, cheat, or steal. Rather, with integrity he led the team to a successful comeback and to, possibly, even greater strength.

- As SUCCESSFUL PERSONALLY I would rate myself _____.

### 26. Teachable

A wise President has a history of having worked with *advisers both inside the organization and out.* He has listened to wise counsel from inside his organization and has invited paid consultants from outside, as well.

A top leader has the ability to *"learn from everyone,"* but not follow *everyone!* A top leader is one who has had mentors and who still has a working relationship with *wise and strong mentors.* He is very teachable in a mentoring relationship.

- As TEACHABLE I would rate myself _____.

### 27. Team-building (Committed)

The ideal President is one who was already leading peers as early as the third, fourth, or fifth grade, and developing the *social skills of leadership in elementary school.*

The ideal leader *attracts strong men and women,* not just weak or average ones, and has the ability to get "round pegs in round holes." He has the ability to see who fits where. He knows how to bring out the best in people by giving them the organizational structure they need to maximize their strengths.

A great President is also a *natural encourager*. He actually encourages his team to reach progressively higher standards of performance. He is not super critical, analyzing every fault a person has or every mistake they make. Rather, he is more "cheerleader" by nature, finding and affirming unique strengths, looking for what a person is doing right, and appreciating it.

• As a TEAM BUILDER I would rate myself _____.

### 28. Trustworthy

A President cannot be considered strong unless *his word is his bond*. You must have a sense that you can trust what he says to be accurate, somewhat objective, truthful, without guile, and that you can, in short, "depend on it"!

There is *absolute integrity from a perspective of financial account-ability*. He is completely trustworthy in this area. You must be able to *trust* the President to be in a room filled with millions of dollars in cash and know absolutely that you would never come up one penny short.

You also want complete confidence in his trustworthiness with the *opposite sex*. Even though he may be attracted to the opposite sex, there is no sense in which he is highly vulnerable to the opposite sex, or "on the prowl" with low morals. There must be a very high, *impeccable trustworthiness in the area of sexual morality*.

• As TRUSTWORTHY IN CHARACTER I would rate myself _____.

### 29. Visionary

Every great leader needs a *crystal clear, consistent, inspiring dream*. A person's dream is equivalent to his "battery pack." Some leaders have a battery pack that lasts for only a day or two before they are discouraged again, or out of energy. Others have a dream battery pack that lasts for thirty or forty years. It seems that they never run out of energy.

A great leader needs to be able to paint inspirational word pictures of the dream. He needs to be able to paint word pictures of "what life will be like when the dream is accomplished," so the team can be inspired to work endlessly in that direction.

A great leader is *offensively focused* toward the future, *thinking five to ten years into the future*, asking, "What will life be like?" "What do we have to do to move in that direction?" "What are the major goals to be reached or problems to be solved in the future?" At the same time, he must have the ability to inspire an entire team of people to move in the direction of this vision.

- As a VISIONARY I would rate myself _____.

### 30. *"Win Big" Focused vs. "Get by" Focused*

A top leader needs to be *"opportunity oriented,"* with a wise sense of when to let a team rest, and when to *"seize the moment!"*

A top leader needs to have an *intensity,* when required, to take full advantage of and capitalize on a unique window of opportunity. He needs to be a "rainmaker," with the ability to stir things up and make things happen, not just waiting for them to happen.

A top leader, ideally, has a *commitment to the "championship."* A desire to move to the top, to win big, or to be the national champion. Top leaders want Super Bowl rings, rather than just ending the season having come close.

There needs to be, in the heart of a President, the ability to compete as needed, but not be competitive to the point of hurting other people. He needs a sense of fair play, not shrinking from competition, but rising to the occasion and "WINNING BIG"!

- As a person who "WINS BIG" vs. "JUST GETS BY" I would rate myself _____.

## Conclusion

Obviously, not every leader scores a 10 on all of these Presidential dimensions. What this profile intends to do is provide a measuring tool to assess an individual, spotting his unique strengths, areas in which he qualifies, though not with excessive strength, and the areas in which he most needs to grow to be a "WORLD CLASS PRESIDENT."

It is hoped that this checklist provides you with an extremely valuable tool, not only now, but in the future, as you recruit, evaluate, and develop growth paths for people who are, or want to be, Presidents.

One final word is that I would encourage you to improve this profile over the years. Make note of the dimensions you see that are required in a top-level President. These can then become dimensions thirty-one through forty. As you have watched top leaders over the years, what are the dimensions that you have admired and respected and would require for any President you considered to be "WORLD CLASS"?

## How to Use the President Rating Scale

The President Rating Scale follows on the next page. It has been designed for you with the utmost flexibility in mind. Each Profile topic is listed in the left-hand column. The four columns on the right are for entering the score for each topic. You can use the columns in a variety of different ways. If you have several candidates for a position, you can compare their profile scores, side by side. If you want to monitor an executive's progress over a period of four years, you can list scores for each year to see progress at a glance. You can even monitor your own progress over the years.

**A note on scoring:** Any score over 8 is considered a major strength. Anything 5–8 needs to be strengthened, but ought not be considered an automatic disqualifier. Anything under 5 is a major growth area.

## PRESIDENT RATING SCALE

| Characteristic Name<br>(Rate each candidate on a 1–10 scale.) | | | | |
|---|---|---|---|---|
| 1. Action Focused | | | | |
| 2. Big-picture Focused | | | | |
| 3. Charismatic (Personality and Style) | | | | |
| 4. Confident | | | | |
| 5. Communicative | | | | |
| 6. Decisive | | | | |
| 7. Financially Astute (Organizationally) | | | | |
| 8. Financially Successful (Personally) | | | | |
| 9. Focused | | | | |
| 10. Healthy and Energetic | | | | |
| 11. Inspiring | | | | |
| 12. Integrated | | | | |
| 13. Natural at Leading | | | | |
| 14. Market Sensitive | | | | |
| 15. Networked | | | | |
| 16. Organizationally Matched | | | | |
| 17. Positive in Attitude (Genuine/Consistent) | | | | |
| 18. Presidential in Bearing, Class, and Style | | | | |
| 19. Relational (with Male and Female) | | | | |
| 20. Respected | | | | |
| 21. Smart | | | | |
| 22. Socially Skilled | | | | |
| 23. Spiritually Mature | | | | |
| 24. Spouse Supported | | | | |
| 25. Successful (Personally) | | | | |
| 26. Teachable | | | | |
| 27. Team-building (Committed) | | | | |
| 28. Trustworthy | | | | |
| 29. Visionary | | | | |
| 30. "Win Big" Focused vs. "Get by" Focused | | | | |
| TOTAL SCORE | | | | |

Used by special permission from Masterplanning Group International the copyright holder.

# Appendix E: Additional Masterplanning Group Resources

## Asking to Win!

This booklet (part of our POCKET CONFIDENCE series) goes in your suit coat pocket, briefcase, or purse. It contains 100 profound questions. Ten questions to ask in each of the following situations:

1. ASKING profound personal questions and avoiding "small talk."
2. BRAINSTORMING your way out of a mental "rut" and maximizing your finest ideas!
3. CAREERING when you, or a friend, are considering a career change.
4. DECIDING when a risky, pressurized, costly decision needs to be made.
5. INTERVIEWING—getting behind a person's smile, and beyond her/his resume!
6. FOCUSING or refocusing your life.
7. ORGANIZING your life to maximize your time!
8. PARENTING to raise healthy, balanced children.
9. PLANNING—Masterplanning any organization or major project.
10. SOLVING any problem faster, with a systematic problem solving process.

In a tough situation . . . ask profound questions, to get profound answers, and make wise decisions!

## Executive Evaluation—135

Have you ever wanted a comprehensive evaluation checklist for getting an objective rating on yourself by a few trusted friends, in everything from bad breath to decision-making? This is it—135 dimensions in all. A very clarifying tool for you to use with those close to you as you let them evaluate you, this list helps maximize your objectivity and concentrates on the positive.

## Focusing Your Life

Often life, even for a leader, gets foggy, confused, and overwhelming. *Focusing Your Life* simplifies life! *Focusing Your Life* is a simple, step-by-step process you learn in about three hours which helps "clear the fog" and keeps you focused for the rest of your life. This great, personal retreat guide helps you reflect on your future! *Focusing Your Life* has been used by over 4,000 people to help form a crystal-clear direction in life. Let this resource help you FOCUS and SIMPLIFY your life. (3-ring notebook, 3 cassettes)

## Heart-to-Heart Series

Whether you're about to pop the question, or popped it years ago, answering the questions in the Heart-to-Heart marriage series will be time well spent. Questions identify common trouble spots in the relationship and then encourage couples to find answers as a team. Follow-up exercises offer specific solutions. Four book series:
- Pre-marriage Questions, Getting to "Really Know" your Life Mate-to-Be
- Pre-remarriage Questions, Helping You Start Again
- Newly Married Questions, Making the Most of Your Honeymoon Year
- Anniversary Questions, Keeping Your Marriage Healthy and Sizzling

# Leadership Confidence

Approximately 3,500 people have completed the *Leadership Confidence* series. A wise, proven investment in your own future, this series is a lifelong reference covering thirty essential leadership areas including:

HOW TO COPE WITH: Change, Depression, Failure, Fatigue, Pressure.

HOW TO BECOME MORE: Attractive, Balanced, Confident, Creative, Disciplined, Motivated.

HOW TO DEVELOP SKILLS IN: Asking, Dreaming, Goal-Setting, Prioritizing, Risk-Taking, Influencing, Money Managing, Personal Organization, Problem-Solving, Decision-Making, Communicating.

HOW TO BECOME MORE EFFECTIVE IN: Delegating, Firing, Reporting, Team-Building, People-Building, Recruiting, Masterplanning, Motivating.

*Leadership Confidence* comes two ways:
    (1) A 225-page paperback book.
    (2) A 166-page outline in a 3-ring notebook and 8 audio
        cassettes.

# Memories Book

Are your parents, grandparents, favorite aunts, uncles, or mentors still living? Then, *Memories* is an ideal gift. Written memories become family heirlooms for your children's children which are guaranteed to become priceless with the passage of time.

*Memories* contains over 500 memory jogging questions to help your loved one relive and write about her or his life's milestones. *Memories* is a beautiful album-type book with padded covers and a binding which opens widely for easy writing. *Memories* is designed to last hundreds of years because it is printed on museum-quality, acid-free paper.

## Mentoring: How to Find One and How to Become One

This 20-page booklet gives you very useful steps about forming a Mentoring relationship and answers practical Mentoring questions with tried and true answers. A Mentoring relationship can easily add 30–50 percent extra "LIFE & LEADERSHIP HORSEPOWER" to any person. Without a mentor, a person often feels underpowered, as if not living up to her or his true potential.

## Mentoring: Confidence in Finding a Mentor and Becoming One

If you would like to be a mentor, or find a mentor, but don't know where to start, this is it! This book explains clearly and completely what mentors do and don't do, the nature of the mentor/protégé relationship, the most common roadblocks to effective mentoring, and much more.

Mentoring is an invaluable way of teaching skills, traditions, and cultural nuances that can't be captured in the classroom. It helps you (as protégé) reach your full potential, and gives you (as mentor) the satisfaction of seeing your experience and ideals carried forward to the next generation. Mentoring is something anyone can do . . . but not everyone should do. This book shows you that being a successful mentor doesn't require perfection, and finding a mentor is probably much easier than you think. Mentoring can make a major difference in your life.

Mentoring is the "linch pin" connecting this generation of leadership to the next. If you have been praying about a way to have your life make a very significant difference . . . Mentoring may be your life ministry!

NOTE: To request a free *Mentoring Today* newsletter, call 1-800-346-1991.

## Role Preference Inventory

The *Role Preference Inventory* (6th edition–17th printing since 1980) is a proven way of understanding yourself better. In simple language, it lets you tell your spouse, your friends, or your colleagues: "What makes you tick!" "What turns you on!" "What burns you out!"

The *Role Preference Inventory* clarifies what you really want to do, not what you have to do, have done the most, or think others expect of you. It is the key to understanding personal fulfillment and is an affordable way of building strong team unity by predicting team chemistry.

This profoundly simple, self-scoring, self-interpreting inventory is the key to selecting the right person for the right position, thus helping avoid costly hiring mistakes.

## Stop Setting Goals If You Would Rather Solve Problems

Do you hate setting goals . . . or know someone who does? Then this book is for you!

"I no longer feel like a second-class citizen!" is the most common reaction to this idea. This entire book is a very helpful part of the realistic assessment of your personality as you develop your new dream for the future, in the middle of your Midlife reevaluation.

As a team leader you can reduce team tensions by 50 percent and increase team spirit by 50 percent, at the same time, by introducing this simple idea at your next staff meeting. Any leader who understands and implements this idea will make her/his team leader, board, stockholders very happy with the results!

## The Question Book

DECISIONS, DECISIONS, DECISIONS! Don't make a major or stressful decision again without asking yourself these profound questions! Ninety-nine experts give you the twenty questions they would teach their own son or daughter to ask before making an important decision in their area of expertise.

- The *Question Book* is a lifelong reference book. Written in a classic style to last a lifetime, it will never really be "out of date." Topics are alphabetically easy to find.
- This *ideal resource for any person living alone* tests one's thinking to gain a more objective perspective before making any decision ESPECIALLY if a former wise adviser is no longer available for counsel.
- This *great gift from a parent to an adult son or daughter* supplements experience and wisdom without appearing "nosy or domineering."
- These questions *reduce the stress of making a risky decision* in a field in which you have little or no experience.

- This *wise investment for each staff member* saves many dollars over the years.
- You *can save thousands, if not millions, of dollars* by knowing how to make wise decisions while under stress, pressure, or emotional manipulation.

## Where to Focus When Your Life's a Blur
by Cheryl Biehl

Do you find yourself juggling the many hats of household taxi, travel agent, correspondent, nurse, tutor, coach, encyclopedia, psychologist, nutritionist, referee, and answering machine? Then, as a Christian, you are expected to participate in your church activities, so you attend a weekly Bible study, volunteer to make crafts to sell at the annual bazaar, and teach a Sunday School class. IF THIS SOUNDS FAMILIAR, this book gives practical step-by-step help in sorting out your priorities and making choices that are best for you.

## Why You Do What You Do

This book is a result of over 21,000 hours of behind-the-defenses experiences with some of the finest, emotionally healthy leaders of our generation. This model was developed to maximize "healthy" people with a few emotional "mysteries" still unanswered!

- Why do I have a phobic fear of failure, rejection, or insignificance?
- Why am I so "driven" to be admired, recognized, appreciated, secure, respected, or accepted?
- Why am I an enabler, leader, promoter, rescuer, controller, people-pleaser?
- Why am I a perfectionist, workaholic, or "withdrawer" from tough situations?
- Why are pastors vulnerable to affairs? Where am I the most vulnerable to temptation? How do I guard against temptation?
- Why do I have such a hard time relating to my parents when I love them so much?
- Why do they sometimes seem like such children?

These and other "emotional mysteries" can be understood and resolved in the silence of your own heart without years of therapy.

## To Receive Free Information On:

- Bobb Biehl's speaking
- Consulting from Masterplanning Group
  Call: 1-407-330-2028 or write:
  Masterplanning Group
  Box 952499
  Lake Mary, Florida 32795

## To Order Any of the Resources Listed Above

- Or receive a free copy of Masterplanning Group's complete resource catalogue:
  Call: 1-800-443-1976 or write:
  Masterplanning Group
  Box 952499
  Lake Mary, Florida 32795

305.244
B5868

99308

LINCOLN CHRISTIAN COLLEGE AND SEMINARY

3 4711 00152 8845